Virtual Sales Skills

The Ultimate Guide to Succeeding in Remote Sales

Kelli Stello

© Copyright 2024 - All rights reserved.

The content contained within this book may not be reproduced, duplicated or transmitted without direct written permission from the author or the publisher.

Under no circumstances will any blame or legal responsibility be held against the publisher, or author, for any damages, reparation, or monetary loss due to the information contained within this book, either directly or indirectly.

Legal Notice:

This book is copyright protected. It is only for personal use. You cannot amend, distribute, sell, use, quote or paraphrase any part, or the content within this book, without the consent of the author or publisher.

Disclaimer Notice:

Please note the information contained within this document is for educational and entertainment purposes only. All effort has been executed to present accurate, up to date, reliable, complete information. No warranties of any kind are declared or implied. Readers acknowledge that the author is not engaged in the rendering of legal, financial, medical or professional advice. The content within this book has been derived from various sources. Please consult a licensed professional before attempting any techniques outlined in this book.

By reading this document, the reader agrees that under no circumstances is the author responsible for any losses, direct or indirect, that are incurred as a result of the use of the information contained within this document, including, but not limited to, errors, omissions, or inaccuracies.

Table of Contents

INTRODUCTION 1
    WHAT THIS BOOK IS NOT ABOUT? 2
    WHO NEEDS TO READ THIS BOOK? 2

CHAPTER 1: INTRODUCTION TO VIRTUAL SALES 5
    WHAT IS VIRTUAL SALES? 5
        Working Mechanism of Virtual Sales 6
    THE RISE OF REMOTE SELLING: TRENDS AND STATISTICS 7
        Statistics That Show Virtual Sales Is Here to Stay 9
    ADVANTAGES AND CHALLENGES OF VIRTUAL SALES 10
        Benefits of Virtual Selling 10
        Drawbacks of Virtual Selling 13
    ESSENTIAL SKILLS FOR VIRTUAL SALES SUCCESS 15
        Digital and Technical Knowledge 16
        Relationship Building Skills 17
        Communication Skills 17
        Organizing Skills 18
        Being Resilient 18
        Having an Analytic Brain 19
        Being Customer-Centric in Your Approach 19
    VIRTUAL SELLING PREP EXERCISE: RECEIVE A FLAT "NO" 20

CHAPTER 2: ACHIEVING PROFICIENCY IN THE VIRTUAL SALES PROCESS 23
    PROSPECTING IN THE DIGITAL AGE 23
        Steps for Effective Virtual Prospecting 26
    THE "LASER" METHOD FOR IDENTIFYING HIGH-QUALITY LEADS 29
        Look and Listen 29
        Ask 30
        Seek 31
        Evaluate 31
        Respond 32
        Applying the LASER Method in a Real-Life Scenario 32
        Define the Avatar of Your Buyer 33
    CRAFT COMPELLING EMAIL OUTREACH WITH THE MARKETING TEAM 36
        Understanding Your Email Outreach Objective 36
        Align the Emails to Your Target Audience 37
        Grab Their Attention with Eye-Catching Subject Lines 37

- *Hyper-Personalize Your Email Messages* 37
- *Make Your Emails Look Engaging* 38
- *Analyze Progress and Optimize* 39
- THE ART OF SOCIAL SELLING 39
  - *Building a Personal Brand* 41
  - *Providing Valuable Content* 41
  - *Connecting with the Right Prospects* 42
  - *Building Relationships with Prospects* 42
  - *Leverage Social Tools to Gain Insights* 43
- NAVIGATING THE VIRTUAL SALES FUNNEL 43
  - *Touchpoint #1—The Awareness Stage* 44
  - *Touchpoint #2—The Interest Stage* 45
  - *Touchpoint #3—The Consideration Stage* 45
  - *Touchpoint #4—The Decision Stage* 46
  - *Touchpoint #5—The Purchase Stage* 46
  - *Touchpoint #6—The Post-Purchase Stage* 46
- THE "CLOSE" FRAMEWORK FOR SEALING THE DEAL REMOTELY 48
  - *Connect* 49
  - *Listen* 49
  - *Offer* 50
  - *Secure* 50
  - *Execute* 50
- VIRTUAL SELLING PREP EXCERCISE: PUT IN THE NUMBERS... HIGH-QUALITY ONES 51

CHAPTER 3: BUILDING RELATIONSHIPS IN A VIRTUAL WORLD 53

- ESTABLISHING TRUST AND RAPPORT ONLINE 53
  - *Personalization* 54
  - *Authenticity* 55
  - *Clear Communication* 55
  - *Empathy* 56
  - *Being Relatable* 56
  - *Active Listening* 56
  - *Delivering Value* 57
  - *Social Proof* 57
- THE IMPORTANCE OF ACTIVE LISTENING IN VIRTUAL SALES 58
  - *Set the Stage* 58
  - *Set Expectations Early On* 59
  - *Acknowledge and Confirm the Prospect's Needs* 59
  - *Ask Open-Ended Questions* 61
  - *Stay Attentive to Cues* 61
  - *Showcase Empathy* 62
  - *Record Your Listening through Notes* 62
- OVERCOMING OBJECTIONS AND CONCERNS IN REMOTE SELLING 63
  - *Understand Their Objections* 64

    Validate Their Objections with Empathy 65
    Clarify Their Objections 66
    Exhibit Evidence of Providing Value 66
    Offer Solutions 67
    Keep Following-Up 68
  NURTURING LONG-TERM CLIENT RELATIONSHIPS VIRTUALLY 69
    Frequent Communication Is the Norm 69
    Keep Delivering Value 70
    Maintain a Feedback Loop 70
    Build and Maintain Meaningful and Authentic Connections 71
  VIRTUAL SELLING PREP EXCERCISE: "WOW" A PROSPECT 72

CHAPTER 4: LEVERAGING TECHNOLOGY FOR VIRTUAL SALES SUCCESS 75

  ESSENTIAL TOOLS FOR REMOTE SELLING 75
    CRM Systems 76
    Email Marketing Automation 77
    Video Calling Tools 77
    Sales Engagement Platforms 78
    Project Management Tools 78
    Social Selling Tools 79
    Document Signing Tools 79
    Sales Reporting and Analytics Tools 80
    Content Management Systems 80
    Customer Support Tools 81
  MASTERING VIDEO CONFERENCING FOR SALES CALLS 82
    Set and Share an Agenda 82
    Do Your Research 83
    Test Your Equipment 83
    Maintain a Professional Setup 83
    Be Present at the Meeting 84
    Make Use of In-Built Tools 84
    Follow-up after the Meet 85
  HARNESSING THE IMPORTANCE OF CRM IN VIRTUAL SALES 86
  AUTOMATION STRATEGIES FOR STREAMLINING YOUR VIRTUAL SALES PROCESS 87
    Automate Your Lead Generation and Scoring 88
    Automate Your Email Communication 88
    Automate Your Sales Workflows 89
    Automate Your CRM System 89
  VIRTUAL SELLING PREP EXERCISE: ROLE PLAY! 90

CHAPTER 5: TARGETING TECHNICAL NICHES IN VIRTUAL SALES 93

  UNDERSTANDING THE TECHNICAL BUYER'S MINDSET 93
    Technical Knowledge 94
    Problem-Solving 94

- *It's All About Data* *95*
- *Security and Compliance* *95*
- *Scalable Solution* *96*
- IDENTIFYING LUCRATIVE TECHNICAL NICHES 96
  - *Examples of Lucrative Technical Niches* *99*
- TAILORING YOUR SALES APPROACH FOR TECHNICAL INDUSTRIES 101
  - *Know Your Product Like You Would Know Your Romantic Partner* *101*
  - *Identify the Decision Makers* *102*
  - *Tailor Your Communication* *103*
  - *Leverage Social Proof* *103*
  - *Showcase Product Demos Virtually* *103*
  - *Proof of Concept (POC)* *104*
  - *Thought Leadership* *104*
  - *Be Customer-Centric in Your Approach* *105*
- BECOMING A TRUSTED ADVISOR IN TECHNICAL SALES 105
- VIRTUAL SELLING PREP EXERCISE: MASTER A PRODUCT AND ADVOCATE FOR IT 107

CHAPTER 6: OPTIMIZING YOUR VIRTUAL SALES PERFORMANCE 109

- SETTING AND ACHIEVING GOALS IN REMOTE SALES 109
  - *Do it the SMART Way* *110*
  - *Create an Actionable Roadmap* *111*
  - *Leverage Data and Technology to Your Advantage* *111*
  - *Encourage Constant Communication* *112*
  - *Foster Learning and Skill Development* *112*
  - *Keep Track and Adjust Your Goals* *113*
- MEASURING AND ANALYZING YOUR VIRTUAL SALES METRICS 113
- CONTINUOUS LEARNING AND SKILL DEVELOPMENT FOR VIRTUAL SELLERS 116
  - *You Need to Adapt to External Changes* *116*
  - *Building Customer Relationships Is a Long-Term Game* *117*
  - *Stay Ahead of Your Competitors* *118*
  - *Practice Leads to More Success* *119*
- STAYING MOTIVATED AND AVOIDING BURNOUT IN REMOTE SALES 120
  - *Have Clarity on Goals and Set Priorities* *120*
  - *Establish a Routine with a Structure* *121*
  - *Treat Breaks as Divine Recharge Periods* *121*
  - *Stay Socially Connected* *122*
  - *Keep Learning* *122*
  - *Condition Yourself Daily* *122*
- VIRTUAL SELLING PREP EXERCISE: SET YOUR SMART GOALS 123

CHAPTER 7: ADVANCED VIRTUAL SALES STRATEGIES 125

- ACCOUNT-BASED SELLING IN THE VIRTUAL LANDSCAPE 125
  - *Step-By-Step Guide for Conducting Account-Based Selling* *126*
- COLLABORATIVE SELLING: PARTNERING WITH CLIENTS REMOTELY 129

- *Equipping Yourself to Be a Great Collaborative Business Partner 130*
- THE "CHALLENGER SALE" APPROACH IN VIRTUAL SELLING 134
  - *Step-By-Step Guide to Become a "Challenger" 135*
- NEGOTIATION TACTICS FOR CLOSING HIGH-STAKES DEALS VIRTUALLY 138
  - *The Puppy Dog Close 138*
  - *The Risk Reversal 139*
  - *Create Urgency and Scarcity 140*
  - *Bring on Social Proof 140*
  - *Bonuses 140*
  - *Prince Anchoring 141*
  - *Multiple Buying Options 141*
- VIRTUAL SELLING PREP EXERCISE: IT'S OKAY TO BE JUDGED! 142

CHAPTER 8: ADAPTING TO THE FUTURE OF VIRTUAL SALES 145

- EMERGING TRENDS IN REMOTE SELLING 145
  - *Sales Automation 146*
  - *Data-Driven Decision-Making 146*
  - *Social Selling 147*
  - *Integrating Remote Collaboration Tools and Tech 147*
  - *Incorporating an E-Commerce Environment 148*
- PREPARING FOR THE EVOLUTION OF VIRTUAL SALES TECHNOLOGY 148
  - *Invest in Advanced Tools 148*
  - *Keep Learning 149*
  - *Upgrade Your Virtual Infrastructure 149*
- THRIVING IN A HYBRID SALES ENVIRONMENT 149
  - *Find the Right Balance 150*
  - *It's All About Communicating Effectively 150*
  - *Unify Your Sales Process 150*
  - *Diversify Your Toolbox 151*
- EMBRACING CHANGE AND INNOVATION IN VIRTUAL SALES 151
  - *Fostering an Innovative Culture 151*
  - *Maintaining a Customer-Centric Approach 152*
  - *Being Agile 152*

CONCLUSION: PUTTING YOUR VIRTUAL SALES SKILLS INTO ACTION 153

APPENDICES 157

- VIRTUAL SALES SUCCESS STORIES 157
- REMOTE SELLING RESOURCES AND TOOLS 158
  - *Communication and Video Conferencing Tools 158*
  - *Customer Relationship Management (CRM) Systems 158*
  - *Sales Engagement Platforms 159*
  - *E-Signature Tools 159*
  - *Marketing Automation Tools 160*

Prospecting and Lead Generation Tools 160
Analytics and Reporting Tools 161
Collaboration and Project Management Tools 161
Customer Support Tools 162
Social Selling Tools 162
Additional Tools That Will Come in Handy 163
Webinars 163
Online Forums 164
Online Courses and Certifications 164
Blogs 164
Podcasts 164

VIRTUAL SALES GLOSSARY 167

REFERENCES 173

Introduction

If you are someone who gets intimidated by the challenge of selling online, then don't worry! I was in the same boat once.

My strength was thriving on face-to-face interactions in sales. I enjoyed every bit of it and had to overcome some challenges when I first started my career in sales.

But life isn't always what you expect. Everything changed! Prospects are more hooked on social media. The pandemic forced everyone to work remotely and virtual selling has become a new norm to get customers effectively.

I will not lie, I struggled to adapt to this world. My virtual meetings were awkward at first, and I couldn't express my ultimate strength as everything was shifted to remote work.

But then, I started to approach this with a different perspective. Rather than thinking virtual selling was going to run my career in sales, I saw a way to leverage it.

I became more open-minded and embraced the change. The biggest issue I felt was that I was trying too much and overcomplicating things through a screen. But in reality, all I needed to do was blend in my sales mojo with remote tools and platforms, and suddenly, it brought me ten times more results than I did with traditional selling.

This eventually led me into a journey that helped me switch challenges into opportunities and I want to share with you how you can utilize virtual selling as an opportunity to not only dominate your sales career but build immense wealth in life by adopting some principles.

What This Book Is NOT About?

This book doesn't just cover only how you can thrive in a sales call. Of course, you will learn a lot about how to close deals through video calls and also have scripts to help you with it. However, virtual sales are not limited to video calls.

Virtual selling involves multiple strategies that you MUST follow to engage with a prospect virtually from every angle and close deals. This includes emails, social media, and funnels. You will be learning about them in subsequent chapters.

This book is not about jumping on a trend or business opportunity that's working, but it's expected to fade away after a few years. I see many jump on the bandwagon of some trend and once they make a lot of money, they quit, and move on to the next vehicle.

Virtual selling is not that. It is a life-long skill and once you master it, it will forever be with you. You will sell anything in any industry or business because virtual selling helps you leverage client interaction and close life-changing deals.

Who Needs to Read This Book?

This book is a guide not only for remote sales professionals who want to elevate their careers in sales but also for managers and business owners who manage virtual sales teams and want to get the maximum out of their personnel.

Being someone who has managed remote teams ranging from technical experts to sales professionals, I will provide practical insights in this guide that help individuals or a collective group of sales professionals thrive remotely.

My experience has helped me understand how to operate effectively within this sector and come in with a unique perspective that virtual sales skills is the catalyst in business success, regardless of which industry you operate in.

I urge you to use this guide as a continuous learning tool where you can come back and refer to the concepts that I'm going to share and utilize them effectively for your sales career, business, and even for your personal goals. That's how powerful knowing these principles can be!

Without further ado, let's start with the first chapter and familiarize yourself with the world of virtual selling.

Enjoy the read!

Chapter 1:

Introduction to Virtual Sales

If my story told you anything, it is the *leverage* you can create in the digital space to make life-changing amounts of money as a sales professional or a business owner.

Before we go on to learn about the whole virtual sales process, the different tools you can use, and how you can master the art of selling online, you need to familiarize yourself with the idea of virtual selling.

This chapter will introduce you to virtual sales, explaining why it is here to stay and be aware of its benefits and challenges.

You can say this chapter is basically going to sell you the idea that virtual sales is here to stay and you can leverage this medium of selling.

You picked this book to master virtual selling and I am going to justify why this is one of the best decisions you have ever made.

Without further ado, let's dive straight into it.

What Is Virtual Sales?

Let's get it straight on the definition of virtual sales. A virtual sale is basically a sale that is done using digital channels such as video calls, emails, social media, websites, and any other digital platform.

Instead of having a face-to-face or "physical" meeting in the real world, virtual selling leverages engaging with the prospect remotely.

In today's era, the entire concept of sales has evolved, especially since the pandemic. There were times when we allured the traditional selling methods such as cold calling, door-to-door selling, and print advertising to engage with potential customers.

But all of that changed and sales professionals and business owners are able to use virtual channels and close lucrative deals remotely. This led to the revolution of virtual selling as it is seen as the more efficient and cost-effective method of selling.

A HUGE disclaimer! I'm not saying that the traditional methods are by any means dead! Of course, cold-calling is still effective, and door-to-door selling can still get you sales depending on the industry you work in.

Nevertheless, virtual selling is a one-of-a-kind process that you can use to engage with your prospect from any angle and increase your chances of getting sales.

Think of it this way: Traditional selling is like watering your garden with a single can all by yourself. Yes, there may be more care and personal connection felt when you water the plant, but it will eventually take you more time to water the entire garden. That too, you won't be able to give each plant the care it needs equally. I'm sure you would agree with that.

On the other hand, virtual selling is like an irrigation system embedded in your garden. It reaches all the plants quickly in your garden and all of it can be done with the help of automation. This makes it much more efficient and requires less manual effort.

Working Mechanism of Virtual Sales

Virtual selling is a calling that we should evolve and leverage technology to increase our selling potential. You have understood the definition of it but virtual selling also comes in two major types:

One is the *synchronous* engagement where you collaborate with the prospect in real time. This is where video calls come in as you engage with the client in real time.

The other is *asynchronous* engagement where you more or less engage with the prospect in a back-and-forth conversation. This is where emails, engaging with prospects through social media posts, and so on come into play.

Familiarize yourself with these two terms as it will make a lot of sense when we cover a few methods in subsequent chapters.

While synchronous engagements can be a great way to build good first impressions and create personal connections, asynchronous engagements are focused on long-term strategic moves you build with the customer to make them trust you more and lean towards buying whatever you are selling.

Virtual selling should always include a mix of both if you want to see the best results.

The Rise of Remote Selling: Trends and Statistics

As the world has shifted towards the leveraging of digital communication channels, this has given businesses opportunities to use technology to learn more about their target market and establish trust with them.

We will see in this section a few trends which have affected the rise of remote selling.

Trend #1: Rise of E-Commerce

While you may have nothing to do with e-commerce businesses, the tremendous growth of e-commerce platforms has shifted consumer mindset towards choosing online transactions over buying them physically.

This obviously led to more and more businesses driving their prospects towards making online purchases and there are payment tools that help you integrate your website in taking online payments such as PayPal, Stripe, etc.

Trend #2: Embracing Remote Work Culture

Another trend that has caught the eyes of everyone since the COVID-19 pandemic, is that the remote work culture is here to stay.

While many would have varied opinions on the effectiveness of working remotely, one cannot deny that it can provide flexibility and freedom to virtual sales teams to work from anywhere and reach prospects.

Trend #3: Social Media Usage

The increasing number of users online has given businesses a heads up that they can find their target market in congregations online, especially on social media platforms such as Facebook, Instagram, Twitter, TikTok, LinkedIn, etc.

Due to the given nature of the social media landscape, businesses are now prioritizing these channels for lead generation, lead nurturing, and establishing rapport with the customer.

Trend #4: Availability of Advanced Tools

The rise of remote selling would not be possible without the availability of advanced tools that help sales teams engage with prospects virtually.

This includes video conferencing tools such as Zoom, Google Meet, Skype, etc. Moreover, Customer Relationship Management (CRM) software has become more pivotal in capturing and nurturing leads, and ensuring the sales team focuses on personalization.

Trend #5: Personalized Targeting

Talking about personalization, virtual teams are now prioritizing personalized messaging and marketing campaigns to build meaningful relationships with their prospects.

This includes utilizing data to understand the target customer and craft communication and pitches according to their needs and online behavior.

Trend #6: Efficiency of Artificial Intelligence

Of course, I can't forget to mention about AI. There has been much negativity with AI replacing many of our jobs but if you incorporate AI into your sales process, then you would be irreplaceable.

Nowadays, many AI-powered tools help to automate the whole sales process and prospect interactions. As a result, it helps sales professionals and business owners to chip in to deliver the final blow (in this case, pitching the offer) after the lead has been nurtured well enough and has little resistance to being sold.

Statistics That Show Virtual Sales Is Here to Stay

If these trends weren't enough to indicate the growth, then I'm sure throwing in some statistics will convince you well enough that remote selling is the future.

1. **Market potential:** According to a Reliable Market Forecast report, the remote sales market is expected to grow at a compound annual growth rate (CAGR) of 8.3% between 2024 to 2031 (Remote sales agents industry analysis report, n.d.). Look at that market growth potential!

2. **E-commerce Habit:** Virtual sales are expected to dominate because of the expansion of e-commerce leading to more consumers shopping online. A report by Statista has forecasted global e-commerce sales to surpass a whopping USD 8 trillion

by 2027, exhibiting a gold-mine opportunity for remote sales. (Chevalier, 2024)

3. **Virtual Tools:** There are more and more advanced tools being introduced. Some of it is AI-powered to make a remote salesperson even more efficient. If you thought video conferencing tools could be cringy, then take a look at the survey done by Buffer in 2022, where they found that almost 97% of remote workers use these video conferencing tools to engage with clients (2022 state of remote work, 2022). Also, in 2020, Zoom reported a staggering 326% yearly increase in revenue due to the demand that was seen during the pandemic. (Rushe, 2021)

4. **Social Media Users:** With social media being the hub to find and engage with prospects, you can expect it to be that way for many years. According to Hootsuite's Digital report in 2022, they estimated over 4.62 billion social media users worldwide. (Digital 2022 report, 2022)

These statistics show that virtual sales have a permanent place in the world now, and you are in for a big opportunity to leverage virtual tools and increase your selling potential like never before.

Advantages and Challenges of Virtual Sales

Virtual selling has its pros and cons, like anything else in this world. Nothing is perfect but virtual selling does more good than bad.

Benefits of Virtual Selling

Let's take a look at a few advantages of virtual selling:

Far Better Reach

The biggest plus of selling remotely is that you can connect with prospects no matter where you are or where they are.

You don't need to drive all the way from California to New York when you can connect with the customer through a video call.

In addition to that, you can connect with anyone in the world, thus, expanding your reach, and that of course, increases your selling potential.

Everything Becomes Too Quick

Have you ever got tired of the days when you need to visit your prospect and see if they got your invoice? Or that if their payment was cashed in with the bank.

Now, everything in the sales process is a lot more quick. For instance, you don't need to wait for the prospect to come to you, and also you can reach them instantly through various digital channels.

Moreover, you have online tools that help in processing payments instantly and allow you to communicate instantly with the customer. This can be crucial when it comes to providing better customer service.

Flexible to Constraints

Virtual selling means that you have the freedom to work from anywhere and also be flexible in your work. This helps to create a better work-life balance for starters.

Additionally, you will be able to schedule meetings and follow up on engagement with prospects at times that are convenient to you and the prospect. This should be seen as a win-win for both parties.

Greater Scalability

Selling virtually is highly scalable. You can engage with multiple prospects and nurture them at the same time, all without being there physically (or online) by yourself.

This leads to immense growth and expansion when scaling your virtual sales process to the next level. More reach equals more potential to close more deals.

Reduced Costs

It shouldn't be ignored that there will be more cost efficiency when we leverage technology in our sales process.

You can reduce expenses such as traveling to a site or staying in an accommodation when you make in-person visits. Moreover, selling remotely means you lower overhead costs such as renting an office space and paying utility bills.

Better Insights to Data

Data can be a game-changer when it comes to tracking leads, and understanding the prospect's needs and behavior.

Besides that, it helps to provide greater insights when making use of sales analytic tools such as Salesforce, Google Analytics, HubSpot, etc.

This can help you to make your whole sales process more efficient when you engage with the customer.

All of these above advantages lead to one major thing... well, two: a) improved conversions and b) optimal customer experience. The former is what we objectively target for, but the latter is something that helps to retain the customer for months and years.

When you leverage technology to personalize your communication with your customers, this leads to better customer experience and they will be more keen to stick with you for longer.

Drawbacks of Virtual Selling

I want to make this book transparent and despite the fact that virtual sales have a lot of advantages, it's not all roses.

There can be challenges in the world of virtual selling and we shouldn't ignore that. Some of them include:

Difficulty in Building Relationships

What I adored about face-to-face interactions is that it was easy to build trust and rapport within the first few minutes of meeting the prospect for the first time.

The same cannot be said about virtual meetings. After all, the virtual environment is perceived to be not "real enough" and both parties would find it a bit tricky to establish warm relationships from the get-go.

It's not as easy as taking a prospect for lunch and having all the time in the world to have a warm conversation and discuss business at the same time.

In the virtual selling world, the prospect's time would be seen as the most valuable and you will have the obligation to get straight to the point and talk about business.

But I want to make it clear that this shouldn't stop you from establishing a career of being a professional remote salesperson or seeing your business thrive with virtual sales teams.

The way to overcome such a challenge is to build a relationship before meeting with them on a call.

This can be done by building a strong presence on social media, providing free value upfront without asking for anything in return, and using social proof to show your credentials and make them trust you more. We will expand more on these in the upcoming chapters.

Communication Limitations

Albert Mehrabian, a researcher of body language, estimated that in a typical conversation, only 7% of it is composed of words, and 38% of it is vocal. The remaining 55% was down to nonverbal cues (The university of Texas permian basin, 2020).

It's amazing that nonverbal cues dominate a significant portion of effective communication, but we would find it challenging in virtual communication.

When texting, we only comprehend the words, and when on a video call, we don't pick up the nonverbal cues as effectively as we do when we meet in person.

Such a limitation in communication can act as a potential barrier and this can often lead to miscommunications and the prospect walking away from the sale.

Over-Dependency on Technology

Another challenge that may seem obvious is that we can be too dependent on technology and other virtual tools when we are looking to sell remotely.

This almost feels like we are putting all eggs in one basket in the event that poor connection, social media outage, and software failure can disrupt the virtual sales process.

On top of that, cybersecurity issues can affect the sales process at any given point as well. Concerns such as comprising sensitive data of the customer online through data breaches and also other cyber threats can lead to legal challenges.

Virtual Teams Struggling to Adapt

It should be said that virtual sales teams can have difficulty in living up to their performance when compared to in-person teams.

The main struggles include team members feeling isolated, the lack of effective communication, or lack of team cohesion.

In addition, the absence of a mentor in person can lead to a lack of skill development among the salespeople.

Virtual selling is often seen as a challenge in many viewpoints. This can be due to the absence of face-to-face connection which will be the reason that every customer engagement usually ends up with a rejection in the virtual world.

However, these challenges can be overcome with the lessons we will learn throughout the book.

These challenges shouldn't be the reason to stop you from achieving your target of being an exceptional remote salesperson or a business owner with a successful virtual sales team.

Virtual selling has more positives than negatives, and the negatives can be comfortably mitigated with clever strategies.

Essential Skills for Virtual Sales Success

While many may think that virtual selling requires a completely unique set of skills, I'm here to tell you that it's not entirely true.

Yes, there may be some additional skills that you may need to be familiar with when working in a digital or remote landscape, but most of these skills are core skills that every salesperson must adhere to.

Let's go through some of the essential skills that you will need to be successful in virtual selling:

Digital and Technical Knowledge

Don't let the term technical intimidate you. You don't need to learn how to code or read complex analytics to assist you with your sales goals.

Think of the knowledge and experience you have mastered in some of the traditional selling methods: cold-calling, face-to-face meetings, door-to-door selling, print advertising, public relations, and so on.

If you are familiar with and have experience selling through these methods, then selling through the digital landscape is not difficult. The only difference is you are using different tools that work in a digital landscape.

So, in this case, you are adapting your sales approach by utilizing emails, video conferencing tools, and instant messaging platforms.

The only tweaks would be that you would follow a slightly different etiquette when, for example, crafting cold emails, compared to cold-calling.

While the latter allows you to have back-and-forth conversations in real-time, the former needs to have clear and concise details to grab the prospect's attention and interest.

The principle is all the same. But you are only making subtle changes in the approach and getting used to these tools is no different from how you got used to traditional selling methods.

Even think of using software such as CRMs and automation tools. It's not challenging to use these tools. Plus, most of the tools such as Salesforce, Zoho, and LinkedIn Sales Navigator, for example, have very user-friendly interfaces for beginners.

Your sales principles and approach stay the same. The only difference is you are using different tools to achieve your goals.

Having sufficient digital knowledge is crucial. For example, if you understand how e-commerce platforms work, you will be able to know how products sell online and create landing pages that will help to convert prospects effectively.

Relationship Building Skills

I cannot deny in a virtual world, there is more need to build rapport and good relationships. Some effort has to be put into that.

Working on your interpersonal skills is a must, regardless of whether you are practicing in-person sales or virtual sales.

If you can make a great first impression, establish trust, and maintain strong relationships with customers, especially through a screen, then you are going to do a brilliant job at this.

Other tips that include building good relationships with customers virtually include putting more emphasis on personalizing your interactions and sales pitches, and actively listening and taking into account their needs and objections.

Communication Skills

Having effective communication skills is a necessity in sales, regardless of whether you are selling in person or virtually.

It is crucial to work on your presentation skills by incorporating the art of storytelling in your interactions with the prospect and looking to connect to their emotions, rather than their rational thoughts.

As a salesperson or an offer maker, you would know that most of the time, the customer always purchases because of emotion, and only slightly, it would be due to rationalism.

In the virtual setting, you have to do some things differently to reflect your outstanding communication and presentation skills.

This includes ensuring your audio and video are of the highest quality when engaging with prospects through video calls, and that your social media profile, website, and content meet the high-quality standards to attract quality clients.

All of the above would come under how you effectively communicate and attract a prospect online.

Organizing Skills

As you are working remotely, there is no denying that there will be a lot of distractions, leading to scattered focus.

A key skill in many successful remote salespeople is that they are well organized with their time and resources.

Having efficient time management skills is crucial so that you prioritize tasks in your sales process that lead to results, and reduce time in activities that simply wouldn't lead to closing the customer.

When it comes to resources, using scheduling tools such as a digital calendar to book meetings, keep track of appointments, and so on, can help you to organize meetings effectively and meet your sales deadlines on time.

Being Resilient

A soft skill but truly something you would need when dealing with virtual sales. As I mentioned earlier one of the challenges of selling remotely is that you will get a lot of rejections and it can be tricky to establish rapport at the beginning.

But if you stay resilient, you will be able to stay in the game longer and adapt to situations. For instance, the technology or tools you may be using today might not be as effective as tomorrow. This reveals the need to adapt to newer tools and showcase your flexibility as a remote salesperson.

Another way of being resilient and adaptable is to be open-minded and continuously learn about the various virtual tools you can use, and the everchanging trends in your industry, and implement new sales techniques to stay ahead of your competitors.

Having an Analytic Brain

In virtual sales, you have access to an immense world of data analytics and information that can boost your chances of landing lucrative deals.

Let me explain how by using some of these examples:

- Utilizing data in your sales dashboard to track your sales progress and determine how ahead or how far you are from reaching your sales target.

- Keeping track of key performance indicators (KPIs) like your customer acquisition costs, conversation rates, and so on, to know where things can improve and boost your chances to close deals.

- Comparing different sales pages, pitches, and campaigns, by conducting A/B split testing, so that you get feedback on which strategies are performing better for you.

- Studying the prospect's online behavior and getting access to industry reports gives you far better insights into strategizing how you can engage with the customer and boost chances for sales (compare that with the lack of insights and time-consuming tasks you have to do if it was traditional selling).

You can leverage data analytics to make effective selling decisions and stay ahead of your competitors in landing prospects.

Being Customer-Centric in Your Approach

To reduce the intensity of negotiation and objection handling, understanding the customer is a primary approach that you should adopt in virtual selling.

With the help of technology and advanced tools, you can understand the customer better and organize insights through your research and interactions with them.

Then, when you clearly communicate the value of the products or services that you are selling and tailor them to solve their specific pain points, they will find it difficult to turn you down.

In this digital landscape, it's a lot easier to follow up and provide support to your prospects or customers than if you were trying to do it in person.

There are CRMs to store customer data and remember every piece of information about them, and also the hassle-free nature of connecting with prospects/customers through email and social media.

All these virtual tools and platforms are available to help you primarily focus on the customer and align your offer to solve their specific problems.

Virtual Selling Prep Exercise: Receive a Flat "NO"

> This is your first exercise to get out of your comfort zone.
>
> This is something you will need to deal with on a daily basis when you are selling remotely—rejections.
>
> Just putting it out there—It's not the end of the world if you keep getting a ton of Nos. So, let's toughen you up a bit to be able to withstand these rejections and keep outreaching to prospects.
>
> First, find someone you know well—whether it is your friend or family—and make a small request that you know they will 100% say no to. If you don't know what to ask yet, then take some time to think about it. You can be creative if you want to.

> Make sure the request doesn't push boundaries that would affect your personal relationship but enough for them to gently say no to you. Practice this with others you know and be comfortable hearing the sound of "no" to every request you make.
>
> It might be difficult at first but this small exercise helps to build a tough armor around you so that it removes ego out of the equation and makes you resilient to keep making requests regardless of rejections.

That wraps up the first chapter! We have covered the fundamentals of virtual sales—by focusing on its application, trends, pros, and cons.

There's a lot of money to be made by virtual selling and you can't miss out on that. The next chapter will walk you through the entire virtual sales process, and provide far greater insights.

We're only just getting started!

Chapter 2:

Achieving Proficiency in the Virtual Sales Process

One of my ex-colleagues that I know always believed that putting in the numbers meant that there was a higher probability of landing a sale.

This is especially true as the more you reach out to prospects, the more likely you are going to get a yes. This isn't rocket science!

However, this isn't a sustainable approach for most sales professionals and business owners. Rather than focusing on the number of attempts, I would put more emphasis on the number of *quality* attempts.

In this chapter, you will understand the virtual sales process and how you can be efficient in prospecting and closing deals remotely. We have tons to cover in this chapter so make sure you're ready to absorb a lot of value that I'm going to share.

Prospecting in the Digital Age

Prospecting in the digital age requires using data and different channels to build a relationship with a client.

Even though traditional selling requires the same, virtual selling gives you an instant ROI when you leverage technology and digital channels to your advantage.

For instance, here are a few ways one can master prospecting in the digital realm:

Using Data to Make Effective Decisions

Understanding your prospect's behavior, likes, and dislikes will come down to utilizing data.

For example, you can use analytics to understand a segment of your audience and collect enough insights that can help personalize your outreach.

Take this simple tool; AnswerthePublic. It's a free tool and you can access it anytime. You can enter a specific keyword that best describes what your target audience is looking for and find out what they are searching for online regularly.

It provides you with an overview of what your consumer behavior would look like with the keywords they enter in search engines to find solutions to their pain points. As a result, you can tap into their psychological needs to understand their pain points better.

But this is just one tool. There are many tools out there that can help you gather insights on your customers. But you get the point when it comes to utilizing data to make better sales decisions.

Implementing an Omnichannel Approach

In the digital world, you can engage with prospects through various channels such as email, social media, content, forums, etc. There is no limitation.

Prospecting digitally requires consistent messaging across various platforms and channels. This is not only to increase your chances of getting a high-quality lead but also to increase brand awareness and trust.

Personalizing Your Communication

Prospecting in the digital world requires a different approach when compared to traditional advertising and selling methods.

This one in particular is personalizing your communication with prospects.

Think about your prospect's average day on LinkedIn, Facebook, and other social media networks. They receive tons of DMs almost daily from various salespeople and all of them are using the same script that they simply copy and paste to others.

Not only does this way of messaging bore the prospect, but the prospect themselves have to go through tons of DMs expecting that they are all not worth their time.

Having a personalized message makes you stand out in an array of mediocre pitches. You can use data insights to tailor your messages according to that prospect's pain points and increase meaningful engagement.

Automating Systems

There are many automation tools available that can streamline redundant tasks and make your selling more efficient.

Email marketing automation, for example, helps you to regularly follow up with your list of prospects and make a sequence that will help to nurture your relationship with them.

One can even use AI nowadays to gain insights and automate their brainstorming sessions better. This can help to optimize your outreach within a limited timeframe.

Carrying Out Content Marketing

Content marketing is an important way to build a brand online. This is done by providing high-quality content (for free) and building a loyal audience base.

When you continuously publish blog posts, post videos, carry out webinars, and so on, this helps you get your message across and establish yourself as a thought leader.

As a result, it attracts the clients you want to work with and when your content already provides value, this makes it easier for you to nurture leads (because they are familiar with you and your content) than you would do by cold outreach (because in most cold outreaches, the prospects know about you for the first time).

Social selling is one way where you can use multiple social media platforms to engage with prospects and build meaningful relationships. But more on that later on in this chapter.

Steps for Effective Virtual Prospecting

The above approaches help you to prospect efficiently in the digital space. However, it is important to know how you can take that first step more diligently.

I've seen many utilize various approaches in a chaotic manner without an intentional plan. Most of these campaigns end up with a lot of budget wasted and a lack of sales.

I would recommend following these steps in order to see better results in your prospecting journey:

Step 1—Start by Defining Your Customer Avatar

You might have heard of this before but there is a reason why defining your ideal customer avatar can help you increase chances of selling.

First and foremost, it makes you understand who your actual customers are and helps you from wasting time and effort chasing people who don't fit in your plans.

A customer avatar is a way to make you realize that you can't please everyone, but you can please one specific group of people. Hence, invest all of your energy and budget in chasing that specific group, rather than the whole internet.

You can make a customer avatar by listing out characteristics of your ideal customer, their demographics, needs, behavior, etc. I will expand more on this with an example when we go through the LASER method.

Step 2—Build a List of Your Ideal Customers

After you have defined your ideal customer avatar, you can now go out there, research, and find out who they are.

For example, you can use a tool like LinkedIn Sales Navigator and enter specific information that will filter your search and find your ideal customers.

So, let's say, your ideal customer are CEOs of a SaaS company that has up to 50 employees. You can enter this information in LinkedIn Sales Navigator and find various profiles matching your criteria.

Moreover, you will be able to see their activity on LinkedIn, and the posts they've published and understand their behavior better. Gather your ideal customers and build a list for your prospecting.

Step 3—Dedicate a hub to Store Your Prospect List

This is where you leverage tools such as a CRM (like Salesforce or HubSpot) to upload your prospect list and manage data such as the interactions you have with them.

This helps you to stay organized and constantly keep up with leads that need nurturing and avoid missing out on goldmine opportunities.

Step 4—Conduct Personalized Outreach

Now that you have a hub to manage prospect interactions and also have adequate information about their social media activity based on your research, it's time to personalize your initial sequences of communication.

This can be done by sending personalized emails or DMs in the social media where you found them, each pointing out the specific pain points and most importantly, making the message relevant to them.

Step 5—Keep Engaging With Prospects Online

Prospecting doesn't stop with a few initial contacts with prospects. You have to stay in the game longer and keep showing up, just to build familiarity and gain their trust.

You can do this organically by engaging with prospects on social media platforms in relevant discussions.

Moreover, content marketing is another go-to way of attracting inbound leads. When you consistently create valuable content and share it with your target audience, you build authority and credibility.

Furthermore, email marketing campaigns help to engage with leads on an intimate level and thus, nurture them.

Step 6—Optimize Your Prospecting Strategy and Keep Going

Use the power of key metrics such as email open rates, cost of ad spent, conversion rate, etc., to measure your progress.

Measuring helps to know how well you are prospecting clients. As a result, it helps you to identify room for improvement and optimize your strategy.

For instance, you can use A/B split testing to compare two different prospecting approaches to see which one brings better results.

Or you can use AI or automation tools to facilitate your prospecting process much smoother by researching the target audience, brainstorming prospecting messages, and regularly nurturing leads.

If you follow these steps, you ease into the world of digital prospecting with an intention. This is just a model to follow. You are free to refine the steps and use whatever works for you best.

I've seen many thrive in virtual sales by skipping strategies such as content marketing and relying on hyper-personalized outreach.

But I would advise you to try everything and then double down on strategies that you or your sales team are comfortable with and get the best prospecting results.

The "LASER" Method for Identifying High-Quality Leads

At the beginning of this chapter, I said that you should focus more on the number of *quality* attempts. The above steps help you get the numbers. But it's all about getting quality numbers or leads that are most likely to convert, rather than being time wasters.

For that, you will need to know how to identify high-quality leads. You can do this by following what I call the "LASER" Method.

Here's what it stands for:

Look and Listen

The first step is to observe your target market; understand the industry trends, understand the customer's behavior, and even analyze the competition.

You can conduct your research by observing what's happening on social media, reading industrial reports, and even attending some virtual networking events or workshops. This can help you identify potential high-quality leads.

Just observing isn't enough though. You should listen and pay close attention to what prospects are looking for. This is critical for any sales professional or business owner. Understanding the prospect's feedback, acute pain points, and needs can help you to align your products or services better.

Ask

The next step is to ask questions that will qualify your lead as a high-quality one. This is a step most sales professionals get wrong because they may not know the right questions to ask or even miss out on a few crucial bits of information.

You can keep this simple by following the BANT framework. It stands for:

- **BudgetE**—ensure the prospect can afford your offer and even has a healthy credit line to do so. Even though the prospect likes your offer and is willing to buy it, their budget could stand as an obstacle in your way.

- **Authority**—Is the prospect the main decision maker or someone who can directly influence the purchasing decision? The prospect's authority is crucial so that you know you are communicating with someone who has the final say on buying your offer. I have seen many B2B salespeople (especially in tech) waste time trying to sell to someone in an organization who has barely any influence over the purchasing decision.

- **Need**—This signifies if the prospect has a need that indicates the likeliness of a sale going through. Understand and measure the intensity of their need. Is it something painful that they are desperately in need of a cure, or is it something that they want just for the sake of it and not that they need it?

- **Timeline**—Lastly, the timeline reveals how urgent is the prospect's purchasing decision. It is better to engage with prospects that have an urgent need for your offer. If it's an itch that they need a remedy to remove it immediately, you hit the jackpot to introduce your offer to fulfill their need.

Simply use the BANT framework and frame your questions so that you can immediately qualify your high-quality leads.

Seek

After asking qualified questions, you should continue to seek out more information that will help support your sales process. For instance, learn more about your lead's business and intricate needs.

I do this by researching more about the prospect's company on LinkedIn and their website to learn about their vision and also the industry they operate in. This helps me to make my conversation relevant to their world and the goals they are chasing, from a business context.

Seeking out more information is a fine way to spot readiness to buy in a prospect and also understand what can influence their budget and decision-making.

Evaluate

Next up, you must evaluate your lead based on criteria you have predefined in your sales process.

For instance, if you have predetermined criteria such as targeting B2B tech companies with more than 50 employees and having more than a $25,000 budget, you simply need to ensure your lead matches to that criteria.

If you have a bunch of leads, you can score them based on your criteria or scoring system. This helps you to prioritize high-quality leads that are more likely to convert and focus your sales efforts on those leads.

Do you see how organized your process has become?

Respond

After evaluating, your response should be to formulate an approach that is tailored toward your lead's pain points and grabs their attention.

With all the insights you have gained, you can use it to your advantage by introducing your offer as the go-to solution to solve your prospect's acute pain points.

Applying the LASER Method in a Real-Life Scenario

So far this has been bookish talk. How can you implement LASER into your prospecting process immediately?

This is quite easier than you think. Let's take the SaaS industry as an example. Suppose you are offering sales training programs to tech companies.

- **L**—In your research, you identify demand for sales training in the tech industry due to high competition and the need for tech sales teams to onboard new users for the long term. You can find potential leads in congregations online. For instance, they might be having discussions in social media groups or you can search companies using search engines.

- **A**—When you engage with your leads through social media or emails, you can ask them qualifying questions that will make you understand if this lead is worth putting all of your efforts into. Use the BANT framework to assist you.

- **S**—Seek more information about your lead. Go through their LinkedIn feed or company websites. You may even come across significant news such as the company recently hired a new head of sales or they are launching a new product. These should be seen as opportunities to get your foot into the door with hyper-personalized messages and give them a good reason to invest in a sales training program.

- **E**—Evaluate your leads closely. If it suits the company's size, budget, and pain points according to your customer profile, then give them a good score. Now, you will have a collection of leads where you can prioritize which ones are worth putting your energy into.

- **R**—Lastly, craft a hyper-personalized pitch for your high-quality leads. Here, you can address the need for their sales team to get professional training for the upcoming product launch or increase the company's revenue. Introduce your sales training program as the solution to their problems and keep following up with the prospect till you get them to book a call with you.

That's how you can apply the LASER method to get high-quality leads effectively. Let's now see how you can create a customer avatar that can help land these high-quality leads for your benefit.

Define the Avatar of Your Buyer

When you define your customer or buyer avatar, it helps you target the right group of people and tailor sales efforts towards them.

I have seen many salespeople get impatient with the lack of sales and enquires, that they end up trying to close anyone they find. This is a big mistake!

Defining your buyer's avatar will help you strategize your process towards focusing on the people who you can serve, not people who you can't serve.

A buyer's avatar can be created using the following details:

Demographics

This includes the buyer's age, gender, income level, education, occupation, and where they are based geographically.

- **Psychographics**: This includes understanding their lifestyle, their core interests, what they do in their spare time, and their values and beliefs.

- **Ambitions**: This includes understanding their aspirations and what goals they want to achieve (both professionally and personally).

- **Pain Points**: These are simply the challenges or problems they are facing, where you can align your offer to solve them.

- **Purchasing Behavior**: This detail can sometimes be overlooked when defining an avatar, but their purchasing behavior helps you understand what steps to take in your virtual sales strategy. For example, understand more about their decision-making process, and also the types of objections they may bring up during a sales call or the initial contact.

Let's use this and construct a buyer's avatar as an example. Let's refer back to our previous example of offering sales training programs.

This is what a typical avatar could look like:

Name: John Doe

Age: 40-45

Location: US & Canada

Occupation: CEO/Founder

Educational Background: MBA

Income: Making $50,000+ annually in profit

Core Values: Open to innovation, and have a growth mindset

Interests: Entrepreneurship, health and fitness, spending time with family

Ambitions: *Scale the business and generate 5x revenue. Have the sales and marketing team work collaboratively and bring in adequate leads in the sales pipeline. Looking to take their business to a level similar to the top tech giants.*

Pain Points: *Facing numerous challenges in onboarding new clients or users. The current sales team lacks the ability and is unable to scale. In search of refining their current funnel to maximize revenue growth.*

Purchasing Behavior: *Pays close attention to social proof (reviews or testimonials) before making a decision, and is more comfortable with having a small trial period before committing to the full program.*

This is a small example of how I would craft a buyer's avatar. From this, you can understand that I'm mainly targeting small business owners who want to scale their business and generate more sales. Hence, I can introduce a sales training program that can perfectly align with their pain points.

Customer avatars can differ from business to business. You might be targeting the head of sales in larger corporations or marketing managers instead of CEOs like I do.

The point of this example is to show you that you can be specific and create a buyer persona that is well-suited to your solution. As a result, you will be able to target people that closely fit (if not perfectly fit) your avatar.

You end up moving away from time-wasting leads and prioritizing high-quality ones that you know are the right fit for your offer or business.

Craft Compelling Email Outreach with the Marketing Team

Next, let's learn how you can collaborate with the marketing team and excel in email outreach. Email marketing is a great way to engage with your prospects and nurture leads till they are ready to buy your offer.

However, most sales teams in most organizations end up doing email outreach all by themselves. You can take the help of your marketing team and send compelling emails to your email list that can help convert your leads.

To write compelling emails, you can follow these guidelines that will help achieve this efficiently:

Understanding Your Email Outreach Objective

Sounds like a cliche but starting each strategic plan by defining and aligning your objectives or goals can help a lot when you craft emails.

First, understand the purpose of your email outreach so that you can differentiate various email marketing campaigns on automation.

Is the email designed for generating leads? Is it for nurturing your existing leads? Is it to provide content so that they keep getting value from your emails? Or is it to create urgency and get them to buy your offer?

Clearly define so that you can know how you can craft your email to meet these objectives.

Align the Emails to Your Target Audience

If you have already done your research well, created a customer avatar, and have acquired leads that match them, then your emails are going to resonate with them.

Ensure your emails align with your target audience's needs, interests, and behaviors. Relate to their problems and provide solutions to solve their pain points.

Grab Their Attention with Eye-Catching Subject Lines

Make sure your emails have compelling subject lines. If they don't open your email, then they won't get to read your irresistible email copy. Hence, prioritize writing eye-catching subject lines and preview text (which can be inserted with email marketing automation tools).

For instance, you can conduct A/B split testing on various subject lines you use and measure which subject lines are getting you more open rates.

Hyper-Personalize Your Email Messages

Nobody likes it when you send an email that is written by a robot and copy pasted to hundreds of different email addresses. Therefore, take the time to personalize messages (if possible, hyper-personalize).

This isn't only limited to addressing their name or company. Take the time to go through their feed or website. Check out any recent projects they have completed or the big news that they shared. Bring that up as a conversation starter and show them that you care about their business and you're not just an average salesperson looking to sell products or services.

Make Your Emails Look Engaging

The last thing you would want is for your perfect email copy to look like large lumps of text that the prospect will easily get bored of and switch their attention to the next email.

Not many talk about it but how your email message looks or how it is perceived yields higher chances of it being read and the prospect being converted.

Ensure your email copy is legible and has plenty of white space in between for smooth readability for starters. Moreover, you can pair up with the marketing team and get their help in incorporating appealing designs and templates for your email campaign.

Segment and Automate Your Email Campaign

Segmenting your email list allows you to send target messages to leads that are at different points in your sales funnel. Let me expand a bit on this.

Suppose you add a prospect to your email list that is completely cold. They have little knowledge of their pain points, are not aware of the solution, and have no awareness of your brand. This particular group requires a separate sequence of targeted emails that nurture the lead.

On the other hand, you may have warmer leads who might be aware of their pain points, aware of the solution they need, but not too aware of your product or services. Hence, this group can receive separate targeted emails that focus more on being aware of your brand.

Do you see how segmenting makes each email message more relevant to what they're seeking? It also makes the interaction more engaging and valuable.

Moreover, you can set these email segments on automation by using email marketing tools such as ConverKit, MailChimp, HubSpot, Klaviyo, and many more.

This is where if you have a marketing team, it can be great to collaborate with them on having these email sequences set on automation.

Analyze Progress and Optimize

Of course, email marketing isn't effective if you just leave it on autopilot just like that. Use analytics to track key metrics to get feedback on your campaigns.

Also, by reviewing your email campaigns' performance, you will know which design, subject lines, email copy, CTA, and so on, are working, and also identify room for improvement.

The reason why it is more effective to collaborate with the marketing team regarding email marketing is so that you receive insightful support from their side.

The marketing team is organized when it comes to developing a solid email content strategy and with you or your sales teams' leads and target customer insights, both departments are going to succeed massively when joined forces.

The Art of Social Selling

Let's take a look at one of the most effective modern approaches to selling—Social Selling.

Social selling is basically leveraging social media platforms or networks to connect with prospects and sell your products and services.

With many users and prospects in particular spending most of their time in a day on social media platforms, this provides a massive opportunity for businesses to engage with them and make their irresistible offer.

Remember that social selling isn't just only for B2B markets but is also incredibly effective in B2C markets.

Traditional selling often provided challenges such as having limited prospect outreach and getting high-quality leads.

Whereas, social selling has completely flipped that notion with its easy-to-access social networks to an unlimited number of prospects and data that helps you to identify high-quality leads.

To understand how important social selling is, here are some statistics according to a 2022 LinkedIn State of Sales report (*Social Selling: What Is Social Selling & Why Is It Important? | LinkedIn Sales Solutions,* 2023):

- It was found that social selling leaders created 45% more opportunities for selling than others with a low social selling index.

- Nearly 78% of businesses that incorporate social selling usually outperform those that don't use social selling.

- Businesses were 51% more likely to attain their sales quote when they leveraged social selling.

If you are wondering what's a social selling index (SSI), it is a scoring system coined by LinkedIn to help measure a business' social selling activity. In other words, it shows how you are rated against industry peers or your network in terms of social media selling skills.

LinkedIn SSI is measured using these four key pillars (*Social Selling: What Is Social Selling & Why Is It Important? | LinkedIn Sales Solutions,* 2023):

- **Establish your professional brand**: Focus your brand on being professional and providing real value to your target audience.

- **Find the right people**: Focus on reaching out and building relationships with the right prospects that align with your brand value and the offers you sell.

- **Engage with insights**: Focus on the engagement the content you put out there generates. Engaging with feedback and continuously providing value is a plus.

- **Build relationships**: Focus on connecting with your target audience on a deeper level and providing meaningful value, rather than just being salesly from the get-go.

Focusing on these pillars provides you with a LinkedIn SSI score out of 100. If you do focus your selling on LinkedIn in particular, it is best to try having an SSI score of greater than 75 for starters.

Besides LinkedIn SSI, social selling is something you must master on many social platforms and networks. It is a one-of-a-kind art and you can improve your social selling ability by incorporating the following pointers:

Building a Personal Brand

Ensure your social media profiles are complete, look professional, and are reflective of what your company does. There is huge importance given to personal branding and thought leadership in particular. If you can stand out as a thought leader, then you will attract many inbound leads and find it easier to convert prospects.

Providing Valuable Content

Create and share valuable content regularly with your audience. This can be in the form of blog posts, tweets, case studies, videos, and even infographics.

Why does this work? You see, when you share value with content that is tailored to solving your target audience's pain points, you build credibility and trust, and make them aware that you have the solution to solve their problems.

Connecting with the Right Prospects

Leverage social media search filters to make targeted searches. For example, you can use LinkedIn's basic search filter to find prospects that match your customer avatar based on the industry they're in, their job title, location, company size, etc.

This makes you connect with prospects that align with your business and gain more insights from their social media activity.

The reason why getting insights from their social media feed and activity is important is because it helps you craft personalized requests when you connect with them.

Prospects like it when you share a common interest and provide some value upfront, rather than receiving another generic sales pitch (which trust me, they always receive a lot of them daily).

Building Relationships with Prospects

After connecting with your prospects on social media platforms like Facebook, LinkedIn, and Instagram, you will be able to engage with them on posts they share and deliver more value to them.

Building relationships through social media takes some time, however, than when you do it face-to-face. Therefore, it is important to stay patient throughout this process.

Nevertheless, it usually pays off well when prospects get familiar with your engagement and see you as a person who is trying to help them rather than someone who is nosey in someone else's business.

It's all about your attitude on how you approach prospects.

Leverage Social Tools to Gain Insights

With social media, you can gain feedback on how prospects or your target audience are engaging with you. Look out for mentions of your name or brand, also you can identify prospect's pain points from discussions you see in social media groups.

This reveals opportunities for you to align your solution and introduce it to them at the right time. You are playing a role of a patient yet determined predator, who is looking for the right time to pounce (in a good way, of course).

Social selling might be a long-haul game compared to other virtual selling methods, but it gives you a huge platform to build a wider reach of your target audience.

Working on your social selling should be done along with your other virtual selling methods. I would suggest dedicating some time to social media activity each week to strengthen your personal brand.

This includes posting valuable content consistently, engaging with prospects' challenges, providing value upfront for free, and establishing yourself as a thought leader in your domain.

Navigating the Virtual Sales Funnel

We have learned so far how you can laser focus (pun intended) on finding high-quality leads, effectively outreach with email marketing, and insights on the art of social selling.

What's next you can add to your virtual selling arsenal?

This is probably the most important of all the sections I'm covering in this chapter because knowing this made me understand how I can tweak and adjust my sales strategy to ensure the prospect builds a good relationship with my brand and buys my offers.

Sales funnels are something I'm crazy about and you should be too, once you understand them.

First and foremost, a virtual sales funnel is basically an overview of a customer's journey all the way from their first contact with your brand to eventually being a paying customer.

From a traditional viewpoint, a sales funnel is pictured like a funnel (no surprises there), and when you first promote your brand to people online, you will initially get a lot of prospects paying attention to your brand.

These large numbers enter the top of the funnel (TOFU) and gradually start getting to know your brand more in the middle of the funnel (MOFU), and once they are familiar and you have nurtured the relationship well enough, they reach the bottom of the funnel (BOFU) where you pitch the offer and convert them into customers.

To explain the virtual sales funnel in detail, here are the following touch points in the funnel that you should know about and pay close attention to:

Touchpoint #1—The Awareness Stage

In simple words, this is the first touchpoint where your only goal is to grab the attention of the prospects. You are putting yourself out there for the first time in front of your ideal prospects. Hence, you need something that will help stand out and disrupt whatever they are doing online.

You can do this by posting any valuable content (blogs, videos, reels, infographics, etc.), posting on social media groups, commenting on the prospect's post, being more visible through search engine results, or utilizing paid ads.

Touchpoint #2—The Interest Stage

After grabbing their attention, you need to get them interested in what you have to offer. At this point, you are filtering your traffic and identifying potential leads.

This can be done by using something called a "Lead Magnet." This is something you offer for free (it can be online resources like ebooks, case studies, reports, or webinars) in exchange for their email address.

This helps you to get access to their email and add them to your email list, where you use your email marketing magic to engage with them regularly.

You can also make use of landing pages to collect their contact information and also make them interested in your brand by sharing social proof such as testimonials and case studies.

Touchpoint #3—The Consideration Stage

The reality is that one prospect you are engaging with probably has a lot of other options to choose from. It's not only you that's looking to sell them something. Hence, you need to nurture the relationship and gain their trust.

The best way to do this is through email marketing since you already have them in your email list by this stage. You can provide free webinars or demos to provide value upfront and showcase your credibility.

Also, you see many brands make use of retargeting ads, which are basically ads or emails that remind prospects of your existence and get them back to visit your website or landing page. This is a good way to make sure you don't ghost your prospect and that they always have you on their mind.

Touchpoint #4—The Decision Stage

Your prospect will reach a stage in your funnel where they are ready to buy the solution but need some work to pull out their credit cards and buy your products or services.

Your only goal in this stage is to convert, convert, and convert. Hence, you can get them on sales calls where you can close them on the spot, provide special offers, keep sending promotional emails, and even provide free trials as part of your package.

Touchpoint #5—The Purchase Stage

You finally get the prospect to buy your offer. Hooray! But you need to make sure this part of your funnel goes seamlessly as well. Hence, ensure your transaction process goes without any problem.

Include an online checkout page on your website where you intend to sell your offers. Include different payment methods so that you don't lose out on sales due to technical limitations.

Moreover, you can follow up with prospects through email by letting them know that they forgot to complete the order or confirm that they successfully purchased an order.

Touchpoint #6—The Post-Purchase Stage

Yes! There is one more touchpoint you need to give importance to after you close the prospect.

The post-purchase phase usually includes onboarding the customer into your brand. You can send welcome emails and let them know the next steps to use your product or what they can expect from your services.

Customer support is vital in this phase so that customers don't think about asking for a refund and they get the best experience that you promised. In addition, you need to impress them more after they purchase something from you so that they stay loyal and repeat more purchases in the future.

Having a few loyal customers repeatedly buying from you is a lot better than going to hunt a hundred different customers for a single transaction.

Now that you have learned about these different touchpoints in a virtual sales funnel, you will need to leverage tools and platforms to get the job done and ensure the prospect engages seamlessly with your brand.

Here's what I would use in each stage:

- **Awareness stage:** For research purposes, I would use tools such as Google Analytics, SEMrush, or Ahrefs to understand more about my target audience and extract keywords that grab their attention. Then I can use these keywords to make content and hook them into it.

- **Interest stage:** I would make use of email marketing tools such as Mailchimp, Convertkit, or Constant Contact to drive traffic from my lead magnets into my email list. If I have tons of leads, a good CRM like HubSpot or Salesforce would be ideal.

- **Consideration stage:** I would like to showcase my expertise through frequent webinars. I can host that comfortably using Zoom. For retargeting ads, Google and Facebook Ads are my go-to places.

- **Decision stage:** To get prospects to book a sales call with me or my time, I would make use of scheduling tools such as Calendly to manage appointments. You can also use CRM like Salesforce or HubSpot to follow up with prospects and keep sending promotional messages to drive sales.

- **Purchase stage:** If I have an e-commerce store, then Shopify or WooCommerce usually takes care of my online checkout page needs. I would rather save some money and go for WordPress or Squarespace and include a checkout page there. For payment processing, PayPal or Stripe are ideal choices.

- **Post-purchase stage:** I would make use of my email automation tools to send welcome email sequences after they purchase something from me. If I want to include customer support, Freshdesk or Zendesk are ideal choices. If I want to create a referral program, I can make use of ReferralCandy to assist me with that.

That's how intervening in a virtual sales funnel and orchestrating how seamlessly your prospect would go from being someone who just saw you online to being a loyal customer.

Understanding virtual funnels can help you to sell to your customers remotely without getting into a sales call with them, or not personally interacting with them.

I have seen many sales teams and businesses do this because they understand the ins and outs of a funnel. Nevertheless, it all depends on how well you nurture your prospects and most importantly close them. We will learn more about it using a simple framework in the following section.

The "CLOSE" Framework for Sealing the Deal Remotely

I will conclude this chapter by walking through a simple framework you can use to avoid complications and use it to strategize your sales process effectively.

The "CLOSE" framework helps you seal the deal remotely and gives you an overview of how you can execute your strategies meticulously.

CLOSE stands for Connect, Listen, Offer, Secure, and Execute. It is important to strategize your sales process in this order. I will go a little in-depth on each component:

Connect

Your first move of intent is not to barge sales pitches into your prospect's face but to genuinely connect with them.

Connect is all about building a personal and professional relationship with your prospect so that everything kicks off in your sales process in the right way.

This is where focusing on hyper-personalized emails or social media messages helps to gain their interest and break the ice. Moreover, engaging with the prospect through social media posts and sharing content that's useful to them helps.

Listen

The next thing you need to do is again, don't talk or pitch your offers. Listen first! Be empathetic and understand your prospect's pain points, goals, and needs properly.

Active listening is a good trait, especially during virtual sales calls, but you are also listening to your prospect's challenges and needs when you monitor their social media discussions.

I'm not saying this would make you look like a virtual stalker but it helps you to understand your market a lot better.

In return, you can ask questions that allow you to understand more about their needs and gain better insights that way.

Offer

After building a genuine relationship and listening to their needs, it's time to put in an offer. This should be a solution that is tailored to solving their specific needs.

Rather than sending generic proposals, create hyper-personalized and customized proposals that tell them that this offer is meant for them. Show that you want to help them.

You must clearly present the benefits of your offer and how it can produce ROI in their business or daily lives. Of course, don't forget to leverage social proof such as your testimonials and case studies when presenting an offer.

Secure

Once you present an offer, trying to get them to say "Yes" can be tricky. You need that official signature from them that confirms their commitment to your products or services after all.

In this phase, you can address objections from their sides and give them more reasons to commit to your program. I like doing something such as presenting a low-risk offer that allows them to commit without seeing my products or services as a risky entity.

This can be done through presenting free trial periods or selling your offer for a much cheaper price initially to break down their guard.

Execute

Lastly, ensure you seal the deal and execute what you have promised. Especially after purchase, it is so important to follow up with your customers and welcome them to your brand.

That's why having a clear onboarding process can help to create a good first impression of your brand and convince the customer that they made the right choice purchasing with you.

When you follow this simple framework, you will be able to build a robust remote sales plan and effectively seal the deal. This, along with the virtual sales funnel will make your virtual sales process go much smoother.

Virtual Selling Prep Excercise: Put in the Numbers... High-Quality Ones

That ends what has been a huge chapter on some insightful knowledge on how your virtual sales process looks like.

I'm sure you are already impressed by the ton of value you have absorbed. Probably even a bit overwhelmed.

But fear not! We will go into detail about some of these intricacies in subsequent chapters, with the next diving deep into ways in which you can build relationships in the virtual world.

Chapter 3:

Building Relationships in a Virtual World

I find that virtual selling is not easy without establishing a genuine relationship with your customer. This is especially true if you are selling high-valued products and services that solve acute pain points.

Since these pain points require a high-end solution, it can take some time to seal a deal of this magnitude. This is why relationship building helps to lower the prospect's resistance and eventually win them over.

In this chapter, I will walk you through how to build meaningful and long-term business relationships remotely, without needing to meet the prospect face-to-face in the real world.

It's a lot easier than you think!

Establishing Trust and Rapport Online

In this digital era, establishing rapport and building trustworthy relationships is necessary for thriving in virtual selling.

However, I won't deny that it would need some work to earn that relationship in the virtual world than when you meet the prospect in the real world.

But, as long as you can incorporate some of the crucial pillars of building business relationships remotely, then you wouldn't need to worry about it. You will, in fact, find the whole process fairly easy.

In my experience, I found having these traits and including these strategies help massively in building trust and rapport in the virtual world:

Personalization

When you make the communication more about them, you have a great chance of building a good relationship straightaway.

People like to be addressed by their names, what they're doing, and what's basically relevant to them.

Suppose I sent you a message saying:

Hey there,

Everyone likes to buy X because it solves Y. I'm sure you would be interested too.

You probably would have seen many generic pitches like that. Your first thought would be, "Well, what's in it for me?". You may even think that this person is probably spamming the same message to everyone. This is not a good approach at all.

But if instead, I messaged you like this:

Hey [Your Name],

I noticed the new product you launched last week. I think it's terrific. I even tried out the demo version myself and I liked it. Between you and me, I believe this product can show greater potential.

Here are some insights in detail attached in this recorded loom video. If interested, my X services can solve some of your Y problems.

We can have a good conversation about it someday.

Notice how this message is more personalized to the prospect. Not only did I do my research and get to know more about them, but it shows how you appreciate some of their relevant work and your intent is to reach out to genuinely help them.

The loom video counts as an extra effort to show that this outreach is specifically tailored to their specific needs.

Authenticity

Being authentic should be one of your top priorities. The digital world can mask authenticity easily. With fake profiles, fake names, and misguiding information, this can completely make the prospect walk away after that initial contact.

Hence, you must be genuine and transparent about who you are and in your client interactions. Don't sugarcoat things and let them know that you are an honest and sincere person to work with.

Clear Communication

Showing clarity and transparency in your communication not only helps you set realistic expectations for your clients but also makes you understand if they are the right fit for you or not.

Ineffective communication leads to massive problems down the road and for a business relationship to be effective in the long term, you must communicate effectively.

You can do this by keeping your prospects or clients informed with updates as you get them along in your sales funnel or even in the post-purchase stage.

Leverage social media and other communication tools to communicate regularly with your clients and avoid ghosting them.

Empathy

When you demonstrate empathy, it helps to build meaningful business relationships virtually. Understand and address your prospect's pain points and challenges.

When you do this, the prospect opens up to you even more and shares more needs and information that helps you to tailor your solution effectively.

Being Relatable

Just like how we converse in the real world when you find similarities in the subject we are discussing, it leads to extended conversation and eventually, building a fruitful connection.

For instance, if you are selling a weight loss program, and your prospect expresses concerns about how they are not losing weight despite following a strict diet, you can chip in and share your or someone else's weight loss experience and challenges.

This will let the prospect know that they are not alone in facing this problem and you shared a story that they find relatable and inspires them to take action and create their own success story.

In a nutshell, prospects or clients like it when you can be relatable. It helps to understand what they're experiencing and also makes you look like a fun person to have a good conversation with.

Active Listening

Paying close attention to what your prospects are saying is crucial. This not only helps to tailor your solution to their specific needs but demonstrates that you are here to build a genuine relationship.

I will dive deep into how you can improve on active listening in the next section.

Delivering Value

To ensure your business relationship stays intact, you must be delivering value to your prospects and clients consistently.

Use your content marketing strategy to share valuable content with your target audience regularly.

Also, when you keep providing value to your clients, it makes them want to stick with you more as they acknowledge the person they are working with is bringing better changes in their business and lives.

Social Proof

If you drove by two restaurants and had to choose one, you are mostly going to analyze it from this viewpoint:

Restaurant A has barely any customers and Restaurant B looks lively with many customers. You are more likely to choose Restaurant B because you see people eating there in numbers. Basically, that restaurant exhibits social proof, and it makes you trust the restaurant and its food more.

Likewise, in virtual selling, prospects look for social proof that proves that you delivered results in the past and have happy customers as a result.

This is why including testimonials, reviews, and case studies from happy customers can help you instantly build credibility and trust with your prospects.

When you incorporate the above qualities and strategies into your virtual sales process, you will find it easier to connect and maintain healthy relationships with prospects and clients remotely.

The Importance of Active Listening in Virtual Sales

Let's now learn about one of the most crucial skills you need in virtual selling—active listening.

As you already know, it can be a bit tricky to pick out non-verbal cues in a remote environment. Hence, when you have the ability to actively listen and cater to the specific needs of your prospect, you are going to be vital for their business.

Active listening helps build trust and rapport, identify opportunities to close the deal, understand the client's needs properly, and boost effective and smooth communication.

But how can one improve this particular trait naturally? Is there some hidden magic where only the gifted possess such a skill? Not really.

Even if you haven't been practicing active listening in the past, you can easily master this skill with the help of a few tricks and strategies that I'm going to share.

Set the Stage

Preparation is key and when you are engaging with a prospect or customer in a remote setting, your environment itself is vital to your success.

Let me explain; If you had notifications popping up on your computer screen every minute, and background noises in your room or office interrupting you often, you are definitely not going to listen properly to your prospect's problems.

This isn't just limited to video calls. Even if you are engaging with prospects asynchronously, you need to remove distractions that scatter your focus and be present in the conversation.

Having a quiet environment for calls and other interactions is crucial. Make use of headphones if it helps to separate yourself from background noises. Keep your work table clean and organized. Having too many things on your work table can distract you as well.

I usually adopt a minimalistic approach to have a quiet and distract-free environment. This helped me to stay present in the moment and listen to the client's needs. Listen to them like a business partner would.

Set Expectations Early On

Especially if you are engaging with a prospect or a client on a call, you must set expectations of what they can expect from it.

This is to ensure that both parties know what the call is about and everyone's time is valued. If you set expectations and tell them what they can expect by the end of the call, this can flatten their guard.

Think about it. If you already told them that they are going to be pitched by the end of the call, they are more likely to be at ease and expect the pitch anyway, rather than being anxious about whether you are going sell them.

This is a typical expectation-setting introduction that me and my team deploy when we hop on the call:

Hi [Name], so in this call, we will talk more about your business, and understand your goals, and expectations. This is more to understand what your specific needs are. By the end of this call, I will get an idea if our solution is the right fit for you and your business. Does that sound fine to you?

Acknowledge and Confirm the Prospect's Needs

Practice reflective listening and this can help you showcase your active listening better.

I will give you an example. You might have seen salespeople or probably yourself listen closely to a prospect when you pick out trigger words like:

I need your product

I have the money

I rejected one of your competitors

etc.

you would immediately conclude that they are the right fit and you can pitch your solution.

This not only may seem a bit rude, but it gets you nowhere. This isn't active listening, it's more like rushing to seal the deal without understanding the prospect's needs fully.

It is important to listen to everything the prospect says to you and once they are done, you should first acknowledge their needs and confirm it.

A good way to confirm their needs is to simply repeat what they just said in your own words. This helps to first and foremost, summarize everything you have listened to so that you understand their problems clearly, and also it makes them happy to listen to a salesperson who genuinely cares about their problems.

You can ask follow-up questions after summarizing their pain points to confirm and showcase clarity in your communication such as:

Did I understand that properly?

or

Can you let me know if I missed out on anything you said?

Ask Open-Ended Questions

Another effective way to showcase your active listening is to ask open-ended questions. Avoid close-ended questions as they lead to no new information being learned.

For example, if you said to a prospect

Do you want to scale your business by next year?

Their obvious answer would be a yes, but it barely gives you insights on how to help them.

But if you rephrased the questions like this

How would the business look like for you next year if you decided to scale it?

This question will make the prospect share many insights. It opens them up to share their challenges, goals, and needs. Hence, you will get enough insights to conclude how you can help them or not.

Start your questions with words like what, how, why, tell me, and so on, to start a lengthy and insightful conversation instead of receiving a flat yes or no.

Along with your open-ended questions, you should always ask follow-up questions to their answers to dive deeper into their concerns and also confirm their needs.

Stay Attentive to Cues

Active listening can also be paying attention to certain usage of words and non-verbal cues. Yes, it can be difficult to pick out non-verbal cues through a video call but you can pick some which can help you understand their body language better.

Look out for nods, posture, body movements, facial expressions, eye movements, and so on, to understand their message clearly.

This can help you ask follow-up questions to confirm their needs and understanding whenever you feel the conversation is going a bit stale or off track.

Remember that you should also reveal your non-verbal cues such as nodding to understand their needs and that you are listening properly to what they're sharing.

Showcase Empathy

Once again, empathy comes in as a trait that can assist your active listening skills. When you genuinely understand and acknowledge your prospect's concerns and feelings, you will be seen as someone who they can trust.

Practice empathy by confirming their concerns:

I understand how that can be challenging.

Yes, that does seem like a difficult feat, I can relate to that.

etc.

Record Your Listening through Notes

Taking notes helps to remember minute details that can boost your chances of sales. We are human after all and our brain isn't our best friend to keep hold of information for that long. Hence, write down whatever you have picked out somewhere.

When you take notes during a conversation, it helps you to organize your prospect's needs better and also they will pick out that you are someone serious to help them.

You can also use your notes to review everything at the end of the call to confirm your prospect's needs and concerns.

If note-taking isn't your thing, you can also record prospect conversations. However, it is important to let them know that you are going to record the call and to confirm if they are comfortable with it.

You can leverage technology to record calls, make transcriptions, and log in interactions in your CRM so that you can follow up on your prospects and clients efficiently.

The above strategies can help you improve your active listening properly and you can build effective and stronger relationships with your prospects.

Overcoming Objections and Concerns in Remote Selling

I don't have the budget at this moment.

I don't think this is the right product for me.

I'm using someone else's product, I don't need yours!

Ah, objections! The cornerstone of all sales teams' worries.

I get it, this is probably one of the most challenging parts that we hate to encounter, but it happens nevertheless.

In a virtual setting, it can be easy to bring up objections and concerns and just walk away from a deal. However, if you view objections as opportunities to address their needs and clarify concerns, then you are going to overcome them anyway.

Your goal is to convince prospects that your product or service is something they would lose sleep if they haven't tried it. With this mindset, you bring confidence into the conversation and back your offer more than you would think.

But how can you overcome these objections effectively like most other successful salespeople do?

Follow these simple strategies and you will find objection handling a much more intriguing experience rather than a daunting one:

Understand Their Objections

The first thing to do is to understand why they brought up those objections in the first place. I have seen many salespeople who I have worked with accept objections without finding out why they said that.

If a prospect raises a financial objection such as:

I can't afford this.

hen follow up with a question like:

I understand, but can you tell me more about your budget constraints? Did you try spending a lot in the past and it didn't work out for you?

Asking questions this way can help you understand their objections better. It opens them up to share the reason and makes them back up their claim.

Do not simply take the prospect's objection for granted. Feel free to dive deeper and understand the root cause of why they bring up such claims.

Yes, sometimes, it may still lead to not closing a deal, but it gives you clarity about whether the prospect's objections are of a huge concern or can be overcome.

Bring your active listening skills into action by asking open-ended questions to make them share more about their objections and concerns.

Validate Their Objections with Empathy

The worst thing you could do when an objection is brought up is to become defensive. You don't want to bring a mindset of it's you versus them into a sales conversation.

You are there to help them and when they bring up objections, you must share the same feeling as they are.

This is where making empathetic questions and following up with more open-ended questions could help.

For example, when a prospect brings up an objection like:

I have tried many similar products before and I still couldn't achieve X result. What makes you think your product could do better?

You can respond by saying:

I understand your concern as we have had many clients bring up this same issue in the past. Can you clarify what results those products didn't bring you and what were your biggest challenges?

Then you can follow up by saying:

However, I can show you how this product brings a unique perspective compared to others and many of our clients have had immense success using it. Would you be open to me showing you how?

Just like that, you can flip the script and make them feel like you are there to help them. You start by showing empathy and validating their objections.

This makes them feel you are in the same boat as they are. Then, you can dig deeper and understand the root concerns and challenges they associate with that objection.

Clarify Their Objections

If you are thrown with many objections, it is important to clarify what's making their concerns a big issue.

You can ask clarifying questions such as:

So is it X issue that is bothering you the most or Y issue?

Do you believe the budget is the primary concern, or is it that you are not confident of the value you will receive from your product/service?

When you ask questions this way, you get clarity from their side on what the major issue is and you can use that as an opportunity to counter their concern.

Exhibit Evidence of Providing Value

Social proof comes to your aid when addressing common objections and concerns. People are more likely to be sold when they see others just like them get results from you. This makes them want to board the same train and achieve the same results as others.

Social proof such as case studies, testimonials, reviews, and so on, not only shows the number of customers you have served but also the value your product or service brings.

It basically exhibits evidence of its value. When prospects see that your product or service achieved X result, they will be impressed and know that this is for them too.

It may seem like I'm exaggerating here but bombard your prospects with tons of social proof to win them over. This will eventually work and lower their objection guard.

Offer Solutions

When prospects bring up objections, look to offer solutions instead of being defensive straightaway.

For instance, if you receive an—

I don't think this product is for me, and I don't want to spend my budget carelessly.

You can counter it with a risk-reversal but in the form of a solution like this:

I understand but I can provide you with a trial period of two weeks. You can try it out and see if you would like to commit to the product/service.

Or you may get a payment objection for a high-ticket offer like:

I don't have that much money to spend on your product/service.

Then you can counter it with another solution:

That's okay! You can pay only X amount upfront and we can do a monthly payment plan for X months to make it convenient for you.

There may be situations where prospects may not fit your particular offer or don't want to be sold, so they will come up with objections like:

I don't think X will work for me.

Based on how well you understand your prospect's needs and know what they actually need, you would propose alternate solutions, like your low-ticket offers (this is also known as down-selling), and counter it with a—

I get that. But I can provide you with Y to solve this particular challenge of yours. I'm also offering it at an affordable price.

Keep Following-Up

Another interesting thing about objections is that it doesn't necessarily get resolved on the spot. Prospects bring up objections that may delay your sales process.

You may have encountered objections such as:

I need to check with my CEO first.

We will get news on our budget by next week.

We are planning to buy it next month, not now.

The worst thing you could do is forget about checking in on them to see if the deal is alive. Following up is an important trait of a salesperson because it demonstrates persistence.

Persistence wins you deals. You must look to schedule a follow-up message or meeting to resolve the objection and look to close the prospect.

This can be seen as an extended version of your conversation to address objections and get them to commit to buying your product or service.

If such objections happen, you must counter them with—

Okay, I understand. However, I will send you all the necessary details about our offer. Can we also schedule a follow-up for X date to continue this conversation some other time?

In this way, you keep the deal alive and have the opportunity to keep the conversation going for a later date.

You see, objections aren't offensive gestures or statements to salespeople. They are opportunities that let us understand more about the prospect and offer solutions that are meant for them.

Use the above methods to address concerns and objections thoughtfully and offer solutions that make prospects lean closer toward buying your offer.

Nurturing Long-Term Client Relationships Virtually

We end this chapter by going through how to maintain long-term client relationships virtually.

When successful in turning your prospect into a customer, it is vital to keep them happy and maintain a good relationship. This is crucial for your brand and also for financial stability.

It requires more effort, but you can successfully do it. There is nothing complicated here as you need to check off these habits and incorporate them as part of your client relationship process:

Frequent Communication Is the Norm

Regularly communicating with your client not only keeps the relationship alive but also does a lot of favors for the clients themselves.

Letting them know about your new products or services, changes in your administration, sharing new content, and so on are a few ways to keep consistent communication alive.

You should look to schedule regular "check-in" meetings with clients to get an update on their progress, address any concerns, get feedback, and implement the next steps to deliver more value to them. You can do this through social media messaging or video calls.

Besides that, you can keep sending personalized emails with your integrated email marketing campaign to keep updating them, provide newsletters, and provide discounts on some of your offers.

Briefly speaking, the entire point is to not keep the communication line cold and regularly keep checking in on what they need.

Keep Delivering Value

There is something about a brand that only provides value just once versus a brand that keeps delivering value consistently. The latter ends up retaining the customer for longer.

When you keep making your client's life better and better, you will be seen as an irreplaceable person or business to work with. As a result, it strengthens the relationship.

You can keep providing value to your customers by sharing valuable content, webinars, special discounts, free limited-time access, and so on.

Use the "Value Ladder" approach. View what you serve to your customers as a ladder and you provide a certain type of value to them.

See if you can better that by providing a solution that solves a more acute pain point. The general rule of a value ladder is that the greater the value you provide, the more you can charge your customers.

Maintain a Feedback Loop

Actively listening to your customers and incorporating their feedback is necessary to maintain a long-term relationship.

You should look to value their feedback and incorporate them wherever possible. Make them feel like they are being heard.

You can schedule one-on-one calls just to let them take the floor share their concerns and provide feedback on your product or service.

You can also get this efficiently done by sending them an online survey which they can fill out and send back to you without hassle. You can use survey-creation tools such as Typeform and SurveyMonkey to make surveys.

You will find it much easier to gather feedback on your brand virtually. Use feedback to your advantage to improve your offers and maintain long-term business relationships successfully.

Build and Maintain Meaningful and Authentic Connections

In all of your client interactions, make it a priority to be transparent and authentic. This is how naturally humans maintain long-term meaningful personal and business relationships.

Be honest with the client during disputes and refrain from putting any blame on them.

For instance, if you or your team makes a mistake, you can communicate to your client by saying:

I'm sorry but I/we take 100% of the blame here. It won't happen again. For the inconvenience caused, I/we will provide 50% off in the next invoice.

See how you are not shifting any blame to them or making any excuses. You are simply taking accountability for your actions. Plus, you are also providing something of value (in this case, a discount for their next invoice) for the inconvenience caused.

This may seem like you are sacrificing short-term profit but you are doing it to build long-term profit in keeping the client happy and loyal to you for months and years.

Besides business relations, engaging with clients casually helps to maintain friendly and loyal connections. For instance, you can leverage social media platforms to engage with your client's posts. Leave them a like, comment, or share their content.

Show some appreciation of your client's work and also the progress they are making working with you. This makes them happy to stay with you and keep buying your products and services.

This may sound a bit corny, but sending them physical gifts to their office as a thank-you for sticking with you for months or years is a great gesture to express gratitude.

Some businesses do this and it helps them to maintain client relationships in the long term. But it's more effective to send them physical gifts and mail them straight to their office location as most interactions are done virtually. When they receive a physical gift, it would feel much more appreciative than if you send a virtual one.

In a nutshell, don't be afraid to take some risks and try to impress your customers. They will show appreciation for your regular checking in, your consistency in providing value, and for making their concerns feel heard.

It is crucial to maintain relationships virtually and the above methods can help you do that effectively. Just avoid thinking short-term and play the long-term game with client relationships.

Virtual Selling Prep Excercise: "WOW" a Prospect

> As you have learned the importance of prospect and client interaction in this chapter, your next exercise should be something along those lines.
>
> Your goal is to WOW a prospect you reach out to with tons of value, that they would feel like they're missing out on working with you if they simply ignore you.
>
> First, find a prospect and conduct some research on them. Take time in this step because you need to gather every bit of

information about their business and identify opportunities where you can help them.

Next, instead of pitching your service or even introducing what you do or what company you are from, provide some value upfront for FREE.

If you are unclear what this looks like, I will provide an example. Suppose you are a product designer and you identify your prospect's current interface might need some work. Instead of pitching your service, you work on their current interface for free, showcase your potential, and send a new and improved version in your first contact with them (whether it is social media or email).

You make it clear that you wanted to help them and there's no catch. Tell them to accept your work and wish them the best to get better results.

If you are selling products, you can send them a small segment of your product for free and tell them they can use it to see if it solves their specific pain point and they get any value from it.

You will find that most people show gratitude of what you do for them upfront and you will stand out instantly among other sales pitches they get from other businesses.

WOW them with so much value that you basically get your foot into the door of their business and engage with them (that's the most important thing). You will find this as an opportunity to eventually work with them on larger projects in the future and may even get some referrals coming your way.

Building relationships is a key part of your virtual sales process. When you prioritize this aspect properly, you will find it easier to engage with clients and keep working with them long-term.

In the next chapter, we will dive deep into various tools you can use for enhancing relationship-building and facilitating your virtual sales process.

Chapter 4:

Leveraging Technology for Virtual Sales Success

You have understood all about the virtual sales process and how to build meaningful relationships with prospects and clients remotely.

Now let us look into how you can make it possible. Technology plays a vital role in making this happen as we leverage high-quality and efficient tools to get results.

In this chapter, I will walk you through a list of essential tools and also how you can use some of these tools to enhance your sales process.

Essential Tools for Remote Selling

Technology not only automates your entire virtual sales process but also make you more productive. It is the catalyst to break any psychological and technical barriers that may keep you and your prospect from being in contact with one another.

A crucial part of being successful in virtual sales is to leverage technology. This comes down to the benefits leveraging technology brings such as:

- Enhancing communication with prospects and clients, thus, ensuring responses are timely and relationships are maintained effectively.

- Improving productivity by incorporating tools to automate redundant tasks, and focusing your energy to provide high-value to clients and close deals.

- Providing insights such as having data-driven analytic tools to study about a prospect's behavior, industry trends, sales performance, and making effective decisions.

- Scaling your sales process and business to another level by having extended reach. Geographical locations won't be a constraint anymore with virtual selling tools that make it possible.

- Improving customer experience by using tools to deliver efficient service and personalized communication. Thus, building long-term loyal business relationships.

That's how important leveraging tools for your virtual sales process is. But let us now look at what type of tools you should be using.

Here are the following types of tools that you need to have in your virtual sales checklist and I have provided some of my top three choices in each category:

CRM Systems

The first on our list are CRM systems. As you have learned, you need a virtual hub to safely store and manage your prospect data efficiently. This helps to automate your sales process better.

When opting for a CRM, look for software that helps with efficient contact management, automating your tasks with ease, reliable sales tracking, and also getting insights on analytics.

My top picks for CRM systems are:

1. Salesforce

2. HubSpot

3. Zoho CRM

Email Marketing Automation

The next tool that should be added to your list concerns your email communication. Having email marketing automation tools helps to streamline your email campaigns efficiently.

Strengthening this area helps you to nurture your leads and consistently engage with prospects till they become customers. Moreover, you still need it when you are maintaining long-term relationships with existing clients.

Opt for email marketing tools that possess automation workflows, segmentation for different email campaigns, ready-made email templates for productivity purposes, and analytics to measure progress.

My top picks for email marketing tools are:

1. MailChimp

2. ConvertKit

3. SendinBlue

Video Calling Tools

Next on your list should be to have tools that help you connect with prospects and clients face-to-face (well, at least through the screen).

Video calling tools are important not only for sales meetings but for showing demos, addressing concerns in your business, and also hosting webinars.

Look for video calling tools that facilitate high-quality video and audio transmission, allow you to record meetings, and also allow screen sharing.

My top picks for video calling tools are:

1. Zoom
2. Google Meet
3. Microsoft Teams

Sales Engagement Platforms

Sales engagement platforms (SEP) help to track and manage your sales outreach. As a result, optimizing your communication.

There's a slight difference between sales engagement platforms and CRMs. CRM acts as your traditional interface where you store historical customer data and information for easy access. Whereas, SEPs enhance your process by utilizing the customer data to automate tasks and personalizing your sales communication.

Opt for SEP platforms that help automate sequences, call logging, and email tracking as well. Analytics is a plus.

My top picks are:

1. SalesLoft
2. Groove
3. Outreach

Project Management Tools

You might think this is not related to sales but project management tools help when you have to collaborate in a team and manage sales activities and projects.

My team uses project management tools and finds them extremely effective. Especially when it comes to file sharing, managing timelines, managing tasks, and of course, communicating.

My top picks for project management tools are:

1. Monday.com
2. Asana
3. Trello

Social Selling Tools

For leveraging social media outreach, you need to make use of tools that help you to find prospects efficiently in social media and streamline engagement.

As we have covered social selling in the earlier chapters, the best tools you should look for should have advanced search filters (a must), lead recommendations, and analytics.

My top picks are as follows:

1. LinkedIn Sales Navigator
2. Hootsuite
3. Buffer

Document Signing Tools

Imagine you finally close a deal and you landed that important prospect online. But when it comes to contracts, you might be left confused about how you can have them prepared and have the prospect sign them.

This is where you should include e-signature solutions into the mix to help streamline the secure signing of contracts and other documents.

I would opt for tools that help create customizable templates for you, allow you to track documents, and efficiently capture digital signatures.

Hence, my top picks for these tools are:

1. DocuSign
2. Adobe Sign
3. HelloSign

Sales Reporting and Analytics Tools

Next that should be added to your tool checklist are sales reporting and analytics tools. This helps you to track and analyze your sales data, and performance, and download insightful reports.

As you have learned, measuring progress is crucial to finding room for improvement and optimizing your virtual sales strategy.

Look for tools that have user-friendly dashboards, facilitate data visualization, and provide predictive analytics.

My top sales reporting and analytic tool picks are:

1. Tableau
2. InsightSquared
3. Looker

Content Management Systems

Otherwise CMS in short, these systems can help you to create and manage content as part of your content strategy.

Moreover, you can use them for website building, managing blogs, and getting insights on analytics and SEO.

My topic picks for CMS are:

1. HubSpot CMS
2. Content Harmony
3. WordPress

Customer Support Tools

To address your customer support, you may require live chat systems in place to provide continuous support and engage with prospects so that you don't miss out on any potential deal.

Look for tools that possess live chats and a ticketing system.

My top picks for these are as follows:

1. Zendesk
2. Freshdesk
3. Intercom

Those are some tools and systems you should have in your virtual tool arsenal to support your sales process.

Most of the tool choices are my top picks from my experience but feel free to try each one and see what fits best for you and your team.

Also, technology evolves over time. What I may share here now might not be working as well in the future and we shouldn't disregard the new tools being introduced as they may help very well with our cause.

The point I'm trying to make here is to be open to new technological changes. Nowadays, we are slowly moving towards using AI-based tools to create images, videos, and so on, within seconds. Hence, always look to adapt and incorporate tools that work best for you.

You will find more tools mentioned in the Appendices section of the book.

Mastering Video Conferencing for Sales Calls

For getting a shot at closing a prospect and making your best impression, video conferencing tools come to your aid.

This is where you get close to having a "face-to-face" conversation and there is a lot at stake to build a good relationship from the get-go and seal the deal.

But this is where most salespeople and businesses falter as the pressure gets to them when they enter a sales call.

Besides the pressure, not many know how they can effectively communicate their message through a video call where there can be situations where one person may talk over another.

This is why developing some video-conferencing etiquette is crucial so that you are organized and conduct your video sales calls without any major stress.

Here are some etiquettes that you can follow:

Set and Share an Agenda

An agenda details what is going to be covered in the meeting. If you have a booked appointment with a prospect, it would be great to prepare an agenda and send it to them at least twenty-four hours before the meeting.

This helps the prospect to understand what they can expect from the meeting and also shows great professionalism from your side.

Do Your Research

It is important to do your research and understand the prospect's business thoroughly before you get on the call.

Doing this helps you to identify potential challenges you may find that can be brought up in the discussion and also understand what their goals can be.

You can do this at least a day or two before the call so that you have ample time to study your prospect.

Test Your Equipment

Testing your equipment before the call helps to remove technical issues that may interrupt your meeting. This includes checking your camera, microphone and even your internet connection is working smoothly.

Ensure you carry out your equipment testing at least a day or two prior to your meeting. In case you identify major problems, you get enough time to rectify them.

It wouldn't be wise to check it a few minutes before the meeting and have a situation where you need to cancel it due to technical limitations.

Maintain a Professional Setup

It is true that you need to look at your best when you face a prospect for the first time. However, you need to have your surroundings and technology to guide you with that.

Keep your background clear and professional. In most cases, you should opt to sit in front of a white wall so that it is free from any distractions.

Ensure there is good lighting around you to make your face visible and also position your camera at your eye level. Don't attempt weird angle techniques that may make the prospect feel uncomfortable. It is important to encourage eye-to-eye contact even through a video call.

Be Present at the Meeting

Speaking of eye contact, when you are in a meeting, you must maintain good eye contact so that you give respect to the prospect and make it a meaningful interaction.

Use lessons you have learned in earlier chapters to actively listen to your prospects and ask open-ended questions to dig deep into their challenges.

When you are speaking with the prospect, it is natural that you may forget to nod, smile, and even affect your body language. To improve on this, I suggest using any video conferencing tool and practice speaking to yourself.

Use Zoom and you can create a meeting just for yourself. Imagine you are talking to a prospect and looking straight into your eye and observing your body language. This is like looking at the mirror and you can improve on your non-verbal cues and also not forget to smile.

Make Use of In-Built Tools

In meetings, you may be required to show a presentation, showcase demos, and even contracts. Hence, make use of screen sharing to effectively share your resources.

Ensure you get the hang of screen sharing before the call and also keep your desktop organized and free of distractions.

You can also make use of whiteboards with annotation features such as Miro to give a real-time view of what the prospect can expect working with you and how you plan to solve their pain points.

Follow-up after the Meet

After the meeting, it is important to follow up and provide a small summary to the prospect on what was discussed through the meeting and the potential next steps they can expect.

This gives clarification to the prospect that you listened properly to their challenges and needs.

Make sure to follow up with email days or weeks after the call to keep the deal alive. This can depend on your sales procedures of course.

Diversify with Multiple Video-Conferencing Tools

The last thing you wouldn't want to do is lay all your eggs on one video-conferencing tool and find out that the tool isn't working just minutes before the meeting.

I would suggest having multiple video-conferencing tools available to you so that you can use any of them for your meetings.

Zoom is usually reliable for me, but if you want to integrate with Microsoft Office, then Teams is good to have. Likewise, if you want to integrate with your Google Workspace, then Google Meet works.

You can also explore other popular tools like Cisco Webex, GoToMeeting, and BlueJeans. For team collaboration and video calls, Slack too is a good platform if other tools aren't available to your team or your prospect.

Harnessing the Importance of CRM in Virtual Sales

CRM systems play a vital role in streamlining your virtual sales process.

For a quick summary, CRMs are important because you can:

- Store every customer information in an accessible location, encouraging centralized data management.

- Segment prospects or customers based on different criteria (like demographics, purchasing behavior, purchasing history), and enhance your sales initiatives.

- Automate routine sales tasks such as follow-up emails, scheduling appointments, and other repetitive activities.

- Utilize analytics and reports to gather improved customer insights in order to optimize your sales strategies.

- Facilitate seamless communication with prospects/customers and also encourage smooth collaboration with teammates.

- Personalize and resolve any concerns and disputes.

As a result, you will be able to retain the customer longer, and having loyal customers is where you want your sales efforts or your business to head towards.

You can align your CRM system to optimize your virtual sales strategies by following some of the steps below:

1. **Customize It:** CRMs are customizable so that you can tailor them to match your virtual sales process. This is why planning on your strategy first and foremost and visualizing stages and workflows will help later on when you add this information to your CRM.

2. **Integrate It:** You can use your CRM to integrate it with other tools you use such as your email marketing, social media, and other websites. As a result, you establish a robust sales environment that improves your productivity.

3. **Automate It:** One of the main purposes of using a CRM is to automate repetitive tasks. Hence, create and update automation to streamline tasks like follow-up emails, updating customer data, and so on.

4. **Leverage Insights:** Use analytics and reports processed by your CRM so that you can gain valuable insights into your customer database and overall sales performance.

5. **Train Others:** Using CRM by yourself is not enough. If you have a team, it is crucial to train the entire sales team on how they can use it to their advantage.

Focus on regularly updating your customer records and always look to maintain high-quality data for making better decisions.

Though my top picks for CRM were Salesforce, HubSpot, and Zoho CRM, feel free to explore other CRM tools like Microsoft Dynamics 365 and Pipedrive.

Salesforce is beginner-friendly and can cater to any type of business and its size. HubSpot CRM too has a friendly interface and can integrate well with other HubSpot tools like its CMS.

Automation Strategies for Streamlining Your Virtual Sales Process

A robust virtual sales process is a paradise. But an automated virtual sales process is heaven!

When you automate your virtual sales process, you are ensuring manual workload is reduced, efficiency is encouraged, and your sales performance is improved.

If productivity matters to your sales process, if consistent follow-ups matter, and providing personalization at scale is your aim, then automation is the key.

Here are a few pretty effective automation strategies that you can consider and add to your virtual sales process:

Automate Your Lead Generation and Scoring

One repetitive task that needs to be automated and scaled is lead generation and qualifying for those leads.

My team makes use of lead capture forms that can be integrated into our website and paid ads to collect the prospect's contact information.

Based on the information we collect, we can then segment those leads. We have lead scoring frameworks in place to score and prioritize leads based on how likely we feel they will convert.

I don't want to forget to include chatbots in your website so that the visitors can get support and the chatbot is programmed to ask and collect the prospect's contact information.

Automate Your Email Communication

Next up is your email communication and this should be automated depending on your lead list and the greater you want to scale your sales process.

Leverage email marketing automation tools to create email sequences for you, so that you can nurture your leads consistently.

Automation works like magic here. For instance, you can set up trigger emails based on what the prospect does. For example, when they download your lead magnet (like your ebook or report), they will receive an email within seconds related to that action. Also if they attend your webinar, they will receive an email related to that specific action.

Automate Your Sales Workflows

You will have some repetitive tasks in between that need to be taken care of. Hence, you can create workflows that automate this.

Tasks such as scheduling meetings, follow-up reminders, data entry, etc., can be automated and integrated with whichever CRM you use.

Automate Your CRM System

Speaking of CRMs, you can automate that too so that you can segment customers based on their needs, buying behavior, and buying history.

When you automate this, you can send personalized messages effectively and also identify touchpoints where you can improve and look to convert the prospect.

Despite mentioning these steps, I would suggest first managing your sales process manually so that you understand if your sales process is effective or not in the first place.

Automation is like a two-edged sword. If you incorporate an effective strategy, automation enhances its effect. And this is true on the flip side. If your strategy isn't effective, then it negatively affects your sales process.

Get used to your sales process first and endure the manual labor. Then, you can slowly integrate automation tools and get used to them. Eventually, you can add an entire ecosystem of automation tools that help scale your virtual sales process to another level.

So, remember, first make sure your current virtual sales process is effective. Then, only you automate it! Otherwise, you will have to start everything from scratch.

I have given my top picks on some of the automation tools we covered earlier in this chapter, but for an advanced view, you can check the entire tool list in the Appendices section.

Virtual Selling Prep Exercise: Role Play!

> Let's give some of your prospect interaction some practice, shall we?
>
> In this exercise, find a friend or family member who agrees to join you for a little role-play. Let them play the role of the prospect while you look to sell them something.
>
> But you are going to this through a video call by using any of the video-conferencing tools mentioned in this chapter. Use the lessons you learned for mastering video conferencing calls and treat them like a serious prospect that you want to work with.
>
> This exercise will help you to practice your meeting etiquette and identify room for improvement. You can even ask your friend or family member to provide feedback on how well you did to make them feel heard.
>
> Remember that you are not selling your offer on the first call. You are building a connection and understanding more about their business, and taking some notes.
>
> You can practice this for a few calls and enjoy the process a bit. It doesn't need to be something too serious that you get anxious every time you get on a call with a prospect.
>
> This exercise helps you to ease off the tension and be present in the moment.

In this chapter, you learned how you can leverage tools to enhance your virtual sales process. Incorporate the different types of tools that your sales process requires and get used to each one of them.

You can then identify which tools are the right fit for you and provide you with positive results. Then only, you shall look to automate your process with automation tools. In this way, you can 5x or 10x your results.

Let's move on to the next part and dive deep into how you can target prospects in technical niches and achieve effective virtual sales.

Chapter 5:

Targeting Technical Niches in Virtual Sales

This chapter is where virtual selling shines. Targeting technical niches and selling IT such as hardware, software, enterprise software systems, and other tech products to small businesses, hospitals, government, etc., is a skill to be mastered.

In this space, virtual sales are expected as you have buyers who are very tech-savvy and don't require face-to-face demos or other selling tactics that were done with traditional selling.

You will understand how to tap into the technical buyer's mindset and tailor your sales strategy towards these specific technical industries.

Even if you are not selling products or services in technical niches, I suggest not skipping this chapter regardless. You can find tons of value that you can use in your sales strategy in whichever niches you work in.

Without further ado, let's get straight into it!

Understanding the Technical Buyer's Mindset

A technical buyer's mindset can be slightly unique and most technical buyers (whether they are individuals or corporations) have a robust decision-making process.

To understand better, here are some things you need to consider when engaging with a technical buyer:

Technical Knowledge

It should be said that technical buyers are well-educated and informed in the domain they are in. They possess a deep understanding of the tech and other products related to it they use.

Hence, as a virtual seller, you need to meet their level of understanding by possessing good technical knowledge and providing value with such detail.

I have seen many SaaS and IT companies usually prefer to hire tech graduates for a sales position rather than a business graduate. This is because sales skills can be developed over time but having technical knowledge does a lot of the work in selling in technical niches.

When you have good technical knowledge and understanding, you will be in a position to have a proper conversation with the prospect.

But that's the pressure one faces when sitting in a meeting face-to-face.

In virtual selling, you can showcase your technical knowledge by providing whitepapers, case studies, documentation, etc., that explain all the technical specifications and showcase your product's performance.

In a nutshell, the most important thing you should do first is to educate yourself well on the technical knowledge aspect. Pick up on technical jargon and feel free to use it often when engaging with a prospect to show that you are the expert.

Problem-Solving

Like most things in sales, selling in technical niches is about addressing and solving a specific problem.

Technical buyers want the problem solved no matter what and they use data to measure the results. In most cases, they are looking to buy products or services that result in a great ROI and provide long-term beneficial use.

Think about it! Why would they want to buy software if it doesn't solve a specific problem for them, causes more headaches for them, and requires the IT team to regularly repair and maintain it?

Focus on solving the problem and eradicating inconveniences for the technical buyer. Align the product in a way that provides more long-term benefits for them after they purchase it.

It's All About Data

Technical buyers like to utilize data for evidence when they make important decisions. Hence, you need to make your sales strategy more data-driven to convince your buyer.

Showcase quantitative data that proves the results and changes your product can bring to their business. Don't shy away and leverage heavy use of data and analytics to show these metrics and justify your claims.

Security and Compliance

Nowadays, security and compliance have become a major concern for most technical buyers.

Especially if you sell in the healthcare industries or the government, there are strict regulations in place that require strict compliance.

Thus, it is vital to show that your product possesses robust security, and compliance certifications, and also adheres to data privacy.

You must provide ample information on how your products go hand in hand with complying with the technical buyer's industry regulations and compliance standards.

Scalable Solution

Technical buyers search for products that not only solve a specific pain point but is also scalable for the long term.

This is where you should show that your product has scalable potential so that buyers know they are investing in a product that evolves with their business.

This includes providing strong long-term support and training for users so that they can transition towards a better position when they scale their business.

The above points can help you align your sales communication and marketing efforts to engage with technical buyers effectively.

In the next section, let's look at how you can identify lucrative technical niches and a few examples of such niches.

Identifying Lucrative Technical Niches

To identify lucrative technical niches, you can follow these steps:

Step 1: Study Emerging Market Trends

Recognizing emerging technological trends and understanding what the customer needs can be seen as a breakthrough step in most cases.

However, most can get into a "hype train" quickly and find out that niche is not meant for them. I would suggest spending time doing your research and analyzing markets.

You can review industry reports to be up-to-date with recent tech trends and market requirements. Gartner, IDC, and Forrester are sources that you can get plenty of solid information from.

If you are the type of person who watches or reads the news daily, you can switch your attention to tech news sources like Wired and TechCrunch.

Step 2: Assess Market Pain Points and Demands

If you have your eyes set on one particular technical niche based on the research data you have gathered, you still need to do a bit more digging into it.

This comes in the form of evaluating the customer's needs and challenges. I wouldn't suggest reading more reports to understand their demands, rather I want you to see the results for yourself.

Use online survey tools like SurveyMonkey or Google Forms to make a quick survey and ask potential customers to share their thoughts.

You can make use of social media filters that were discussed in the earlier chapters to find your ideal customer profile and have them share their answers with you.

With such data at your helm, you will get clarity on the customer's pain points and demands.

Step 3: Recognize Emerging Tech

After recognizing a potentially lucrative niche and understanding more about the customer's needs, it's time to introduce a tech solution to solve their pain points.

This is where it is important to stay updated with technological trends and identify a solution that can be used as a bridge to solve the customer's challenges.

You can identify such tech solutions by monitoring sources like innovation hubs, startup accelerators, and tech business incubators.

If you want something extra, you can access patent databases like Google Patents to identify what new technologies are available that fit into your specific market's requirements.

Step 4: Analyze the Competition

Conducting a competitive analysis is a good way to know if the market is lucrative or not. For instance, I have seen many niches way down to the extent that they are targeting blue oceans. But this is not a sustainable approach.

Even if that particular niche may have less competition, it doesn't justify the sustainability of the market's demands. Niching way down is not a profitable approach.

Hence, niche to an extent where competition is still healthy and you get plenty of insights from competitors. You can understand from competitors which niches they're focusing their resources on and also estimate how successful they are.

The success rate in a market is an important component for me when I do my research from a risk management point of view. It measures how likely you are going to be successful and profitable in a market despite going through rough patches and other challenges.

Moreover, you can conduct a SWOT analysis focusing on the market's Strengths, Weaknesses, Opportunities, and Threats to assess potential gaps in the market and align your solution to close that gap.

Step 5: Leverage Your Virtual Sales Ecosystem

After identifying and assessing your specific lucrative technical niche, it's time to leverage your resources.

Utilize CRM systems to analyze prospect data and understand their requirements and market trends. Use social media platforms and email marketing to keep engaging with the market and get more insights.

Use data analytics to get insightful data to use to predict your revenue and potential sales. As a result, you will be able to align your virtual sales strategy to cater to market gaps and serve your technical niche.

Examples of Lucrative Technical Niches

Let's now look at some examples of lucrative technical niches that you can consider diving your head into and learning more about:

Cybersecurity Solutions

Cybersecurity solutions include data security, encryption, network security, access control, antivirus, disaster recovery, IoT security, etc.

It's a lucrative technical niche because more and more cyber threats are being exposed to small businesses, financial institutions, healthcare providers, and the government.

The need to invest in cybersecurity to protect their tech infrastructure and data has become a necessity.

SaaS (Software as a Service) and Cloud

SaaS and Cloud computing are basically what you would heavily rely on for your virtual sales strategy and other business tasks. Therefore, this means other businesses and institutions demand the same.

With most shifting towards remote work and going completely digital, the need for cloud services has become an integral part of their work process.

Hence, small businesses, large enterprises, educational institutions, government agencies, and so on, require them to cater to day-to-day needs.

Artificial Intelligence and Machine Learning Solutions

From speech, and image recognition to virtual personal assistants, AI and ML are revolutionizing many industries with their applications.

It is a lucrative technical niche because the need for automation and improving on making important decisions has become crucial to optimize customer experience and succeed in this competitive world.

AI and ML solutions cater well to tech companies, the healthcare industry, manufacturing, retail, financial services, and so on.

Internet of Things (IoT) Applications

IoT enables smart devices and other systems to effectively reduce costs for organizations, and maximize their working productivity.

It is lucrative as more and more businesses and institutions are looking to create efficient business infrastructure to maximize their output.

Be it for manufacturing, healthcare, retail, and so on, IoT solutions are needed to stay connected and create synergy.

5G Technology

The emerging 5G is here to enhance communication lines by providing faster and more stable connectivity.

You will find this niche lucrative as many telecommunication companies, tech developers, and smart city planners look to implement 5G technology into their infrastructure.

Telemedicine

Ever since the recent pandemic, there has been immense growth in telemedicine and digital health solutions.

Telemedicine basically refers to remote clinical services between the healthcare provider and the patient, only done virtually rather than physically.

This niche will see good growth as more hospitals, clinics, and other healthcare providers are integrating telemedicine services into their daily processes.

These were some examples of lucrative technical niches that you can explore and learn more about. In the next section, I will walk you through how you can tailor your sales strategy for such technical industries.

Tailoring Your Sales Approach for Technical Industries

Let's now learn how you can align your virtual sales approach and dominate your specific technical niche.

First things first! How well you have done your research will determine how successful you can be in selling in your market. I'm not saying this lightly either.

Spend more time and understanding the market or industry you are in. Keep absorbing reports, blogs, articles, and collect data from surveys to understand more about the customer's needs.

A great way to dominate a technical market is to find unique challenges faced by your target market and look to introduce a solution that helps solve them.

Now, let's go through the next steps and strategies that you can incorporate into your virtual sales approach:

Know Your Product Like You Would Know Your Romantic Partner

I'm not exaggerating here.

You need to understand your tech solution thoroughly and showcase yourself as an expert to pitch that product.

Remember when we talked about the need to have technical knowledge? Your target customers are going to have good technical knowledge and know what they are dealing with. You must match their level.

Understand your solution's technical specifications, pros, and cons, and be an expert in articulately communicating the benefits and use cases of your product to technical buyers.

Identify the Decision Makers

Alright, unlike other niches, you are mostly going to target large enterprises, institutions, and organizations in the technical niche.

Hence, you need a robust plan to identify and engage with key decision-makers. I stress on key because they are the ones that will help you move the deal along, for the better or the worse.

You don't want to engage with someone in an organization who has no influence on making purchasing decisions and end up wasting your time. Time is valuable that it could've been used elsewhere on more important leads.

Create a chart of key stakeholders you identify when you look to sell your solutions. This can vary from organization to organization, but most key decision-makers include IT managers, CTOs, and other technical bosses.

After identifying and engaging with such key decision-makers, understand clearly their roles and influence on the decision-making so that you know they are the right people to engage with and get the deal moving in the right direction.

Tailor Your Communication

Personalizing your message comes to your aid in the technical industry too.

Additionally, you must showcase your technical knowledge by including the usage of industry-specific terminology and basic technical language that your target customers can closely resonate with.

Tailor your marketing and sales message in such a way that it closely focuses on the specific needs and challenges that your target customer is suffering from.

Leverage Social Proof

Even in the technical industry, social proof can buy you deals. It's become a necessity to show them that your product will solve their specific need.

Hence, you need to present them with case studies and testimonials from satisfied customers in the relevant industry to showcase credibility. Plus, it's all about building that trust!

Showcase Product Demos Virtually

Leverage virtual channels to meet up with your customers and present detailed technical product demos.

This way, you can clearly show them the features and capabilities your product possesses and also show them live on how it solves that specific problem.

During these demos, you can even ask them if they have any questions to address their concerns and objections they may have regarding your product.

Proof of Concept (POC)

In most cases, demos showcase the idea but the actual proof is when the target customer themselves are using the product and solving their challenges.

Of course, you can't easily just sell them the tech solution and expect them to be happy with it or not. This is where providing free trials or versions comes into play.

There is a phenomenon known as "product-led" growth. This is where the product does all the selling for you. You provide a free trial for a limited time to your customers to use the product and see if it helps them solve their problems.

In this way, customers can get a good taste of your product and will pay the full price to get permanent access to it.

Free trials and plans are something that you see often with SaaS businesses. They offer a free plan with limited features and allow users to access and use it for 30 days or a couple of weeks.

After the use customers develop an emotional attachment to the tool because it solves their specific needs effortlessly making them more efficient, they show little resistance to upgrade to a paid plan.

Likewise, this can be applied in other technical niches. Simply provide a limited version of your solution as a free trial to target customers and let your product convince them to pay the big bucks later on.

Thought Leadership

When you position your business as a thought leader in a specific industry, you have a better chance of attracting more leads your way.

Let's face it! You could be in a market where your competitors offer the same solution as you do. So, what can you do to stand out and cut through all that competition?

Simple. You establish yourself as the go-to person. And how can one do this? Exactly! by creating and sharing valuable educational content with your target audience.

Leverage content marketing to consistently provide value and build a huge audience where you can get good word-of-mouth and inbound leads.

Besides content marketing, look to participate in your specific industry's online forums, online workshops, and conferences to establish yourself as a thought leader.

Be Customer-Centric in Your Approach

For technical solutions especially, taking a customer-centric approach helps you to build sustainable and long-term relationships.

Think about big tech brands like Apple, Microsoft, and so on. Why do they keep succeeding? Because they adopt a customer-centric approach, keep listening to their customer's needs, and tailor their solutions to always meet those needs consistently.

Therefore, focus on those unique needs and always look to solve them. Keep engaging with your customers through emails, calls, and so on, to establish rapport and actively listen to their challenges.

Utilize your CRM systems to track and manage relationships and customer insights so that you can transfer information to the product team to optimize the solution better.

Becoming a Trusted Advisor in Technical Sales

Earlier, we have learned how it can take some convincing to tap into a technical buyer's mindset.

When you showcase yourself as a trusted advisor in the technical sales domain, you will find it easier to overcome customer buying resistance and build meaningful long-term relationships with them.

It is important to focus on this because trust is the foundation of all technical sales. As you know, buyers go through a lot of pressure because it is significantly a high-stakes situation to invest in technical solutions. Compare that to buying clothing through e-commerce sites, the stakes are nothing there.

So, building trust should be the foundation, and technical buyers instantly trust a salesperson who exhibits such technical knowledge and is passionate about solving their specific challenge.

Moreover, building long-term relationships in technical sales goes beyond transactions. You should see your customer as a long-term business partner. This leads to loyalty in the long term and more repeated transactions. Happy days to you!

Furthermore, the more you keep your customers happy, the more you will realize that they are your best sales team as well. Very happy customers are the best advocates to refer your business to others and even get positive testimonials as a result.

In a nutshell, you can see how important it is to be that person who understands the customer's specific needs, so it allows you to offer tailored technical solutions to meet their needs effortlessly.

Be a problem solver rather than a seller. This will help you stand out in a crowded market in any technical industry you are in. Focus on adding value consistently.

Now, how can you develop such a mindset and become a trusted advisor?

I will be brief here since we have already discussed these traits in earlier chapters, but in a nutshell:

- Be a knowledgeable expert in your industry (be open to learning and staying updated on changes).

- Develop a deep understanding and connection with your product (this also means that you should be an expert using it yourself).

- Actively listen to your customers and empathize.

- Provide valuable insights, recommendations, and advice like a thought leader should (do this for free through your content and free consultation calls).

- Be authentic and transparent with how you communicate your message (Simply set realistic expectations about your product, showcasing its benefits and also flaws).

- Commit to your promises, and don't mislead (look to underpromise and overdeliver for better results).

Virtual Selling Prep Exercise: Master a Product and Advocate for It

In this exercise, pick a random tech solution that you have never used before. Pick something that you would feel interested in using regularly and be absorbed by its application.

For instance, this could be an AI image recognition tool, online whiteboard, graphic designing tool, online database management tool, or even a simple document accessing tool.

Once you have chosen your tool, use it properly as you would do for day-to-day tasks. Use all of the features available to you and understand the benefits and limitations of the product. Be creative and use it for different situations so you can understand the product in and out.

Use this tool for at least two weeks. Dedicate a few minutes per day to get used to the tool. After two weeks, prepare a report on

> how well this product has helped solve specific problems, identify areas for improvement, and summarize your findings in one place.
>
> Use that report to remember all your key findings about the product because, after that, you are going to convince **ONE** person you know to use this product. This person may already be using another substitute tool to solve a similar need, but your task is to convince the person to stop using that tool and go with the product you have been using instead.
>
> This exercise helps you to showcase your technical knowledge, understand how to tap into the customer's pain points and align your communication to address those needs.
>
> **Good luck!**

To dominate in technical sales, becoming a trusted advisor or thought leader can help you attract leads and build long-term relationships with customers.

Even if you are not operating in a technical niche, the lessons you have learned from this chapter can help you implement your virtual sales strategy and get effective results.

Speaking of results, setting reasonable goals and expectations is one way to optimize your virtual sales performance. In the next chapter, we are going to dive deep into this.

Chapter 6:

Optimizing Your Virtual Sales Performance

When you establish a robust virtual sales strategy and start engaging with prospects and clients, it is vital to measure your performance.

The last thing you would need is to implement the strategies you have learned and can't figure out why you are not hitting your sales targets.

In this chapter, you will learn how to set goals, measure virtual sales metrics, improve your virtual selling skills, and stay motivated in the long run to optimize your performance.

Setting and Achieving Goals in Remote Sales

I cannot move forward without saying that goals give you a direction—a purpose!

Without goals, your virtual sales process will be directionless and you won't even know if you are growing or stagnating.

Remote salespeople and teams require structured goals to stay motivated and focus their eyes on the prize.

Here is how you can implement a structured approach to establishing and achieving goals for optimal virtual sales performance:

Do it the SMART Way

Some may think SMART goals aren't effective or talked too much about, but I have a different opinion. SMART goals were how my remote sales team got things going and we moved in the right direction—achieving a lot of success.

SMART goals give you that headstart in facilitating a smooth process in your sales team and even other organizational affairs. Once you get used to the idea of SMART goals, you can then make use of other goal-structured approaches that better suit your needs and resources.

SMART goals are basically:

Specific: They define clearly what you are setting your eyes on.

Measurable: They require definitive criteria you can use to measure progress.

Achievable: They require establishing realistic goals based on your resources and capabilities.

Relevant: They ensure your goals align with your business goals, making them relevant.

Time-bound: They give you a timeline that needs you to achieve your goals.

Some relevant SMART goals examples can be:

Increase our monthly sales by 25% within the next quarter

Target a new market segment to increase sales for our hardware product line within the next six months

Scale our current e-commerce store sales from $100,000 per month to $300,000 per month by the next financial year

Create an Actionable Roadmap

After establishing goals using the SMART approach, it's time to create a roadmap for each goal.

A roadmap helps you break down your established goals into actionable steps so that you have a structured plan to achieve them and don't feel overwhelmed by the magnitude of the task.

A roadmap also helps in defining milestones and assigning specific tasks to others based on their capabilities.

For example, a roadmap for the goal—

Increase our monthly sales by 25% within the next quarter

—can be:

Week 1: Conduct research on potential new market segments to target.

Week 2: Assemble at least 100-200 leads of the new segment into our CRM systems.

Week 3: Prepare lead magnet and opt-in at least 100 prospects into our email list.

Weeks 4-6: Launch email campaigns to our leads.

Weeks 7-9: Retarget email campaigns and reach out to leads through social media channels.

You get the idea!

Leverage Data and Technology to Your Advantage

Use your CRM systems to your advantage to get insights on analytics and manage sales activities. This helps to measure and optimize your performance better and get closer to achieving your set goals.

We will discuss different KPIs and metrics you need to pay attention to later in the chapter.

Moreover, when you use automation tools such as automating your email sequences, appointment scheduling, and other repetitive tasks, it helps you to streamline workflows and focus your energy on quality customer interactions.

Encourage Constant Communication

When you regularly check in with your prospects or customers, this increases the likelihood of achieving your goals. Your sales are there to be won in the follow-ups. It's all about the constant interaction between you and the client.

Schedule regular meetings and encourage open communication. You will receive valuable feedback and this helps to address many of their concerns and challenges.

Likewise, this can be said for remote sales teams. When you hold virtual meetings every week to review goals and check on the progress of these goals, you are making sure the team is heading in the right direction.

Foster Learning and Skill Development

Be open to participating in training and development programs to enhance your sales skills and your teams.

It will be important to adapt your selling techniques and tools over time to an ever-changing market and with more competition, you need better creativity and skills to overcome and keep being successful in selling.

We will cover more about this later in the chapter as well.

Keep Track and Adjust Your Goals

Monitor your goals and conduct frequent reviews to measure the progress. This helps you identify room for improvement and be flexible wherever possible.

I will give you an example. You cannot simply implement a specific virtual selling strategy and expect it to work like magic on autopilot.

The initial target market you are exploring may not be responding well to your message as you thought you would. Hence, you may need to pivot to a different new market segment.

The email marketing campaign may not be giving you the responses or conversions you need. This may require you to assess the email copy, frequency of emails sent, subject lines, etc.

As you see, when you monitor your goals and identify if you are heading in the right direction or not, then you will be able to know whether to keep your strategy, pivot to a new one, or discard the existing one.

When you define clear goals, create a roadmap with actionable steps, and use your virtual ecosystem, you can optimize your virtual sales performance and stay extremely focused on achieving any business goal.

Measuring and Analyzing Your Virtual Sales Metrics

As mentioned earlier, measuring your virtual sales performance comes down with a little help from metrics! Analyzing these virtual sales metrics helps you to understand your current performance, and make effective decisions, all thanks to data.

The truth is there are a lot of metrics you see nowadays that many virtual sales teams use and in my opinion, it's not worth tracking that many unless it aligns with your goals and strategy.

Some metrics are sometimes misleading and not worth spending time tracking. For example, website traffic or visitors. The number doesn't determine whether you are performing well or not. The quality of traffic you drive matters more.

Are you bringing the right kind of traffic that fits your ideal customer profile? Is it warm traffic you are bringing in or a cold one? Hence, I wouldn't waste time on such metrics.

That being said, here's a list of key virtual sales metrics that can help you measure your goals thoroughly:

- **Number of leads generated:** The total number of new leads you acquire within a specific timeframe.

- **Lead source:** Where your lead comes from. For example, if your leads are coming from social media platforms, emails, webinars, etc. You can use this metric to allocate your budget and resources efficiently to the most effective lead sources.

- **Conversion rate:** This can be the percentage of leads that convert into paying customers. You can use it to identify stages in your funnel or sales communication where the lead eventually disengages from your business.

- **Lead response time:** The average time it takes to respond to a new lead. Ideally, you would want to shorten your response times in order to see an increase in conversion rates.

- **Sales cycle length:** The average time it takes to close a prospect from initial contact to when they purchase. You can use this metric to identify redundant phases and streamline your virtual sales process.

- **Win rate:** This is the percentage of deals closed versus the total number of opportunities. This metric can be useful to assess the performance of team members in your sales team.

- **Average deal size:** This is the average revenue you generate per closed deal.

- **Customer Acquisition Cost (CAC):** The total number of marketing and sales expenses you incur for each new number of customers you acquire. This metric helps you to adjust your marketing and sales efforts to reduce costs and stay efficient in acquiring customers.

- **Customer Lifetime Value (CLV):** This is basically an accumulation of a customer's average purchasing value, purchasing frequency, and average lifespan. You can use this metric to launch loyalty programs or optimize your customer experience to increase CLV in the long run.

- **Monthly Recurring Revenue (MRR):** This is the revenue generated from monthly subscriptions. This metric can be the bloodline to your business if you are selling with MRR deals. You can also use MRR to forecast performance and growth (for business investment decisions).

- **Email open and click-through rates:** This measures the number of times your email gets opened and your CTA gets clicked. A low email open rate suggests you need to work on the subject line, whereas a low click-through rate suggests you need to work on the email copy.

- **Customer churn rate:** This is the number of customers you lose versus the total number of customers you have. You measure this metric over a specific period. High churn rates are an alarming sign and a calling for you to implement retention strategies and enhance your customer experience.

That's all you would need to measure your virtual sales performance. I believe less is more. Of course, you can use additional metrics if it suits your business and strategy, but this is a good start that any business can use.

Make use of your CRM systems, analytics interface, sales automation tools, and even financial accounting tools like Quickbooks, Zoho, or Xero, to monitor metrics and measure your success.

Continuous Learning and Skill Development for Virtual Sellers

Being open to learning and improving on your skills is not only needed for improving on your virtual sales performance but also for staying competitive and achieving success in your field.

Let's admit it! The world keeps evolving and a dynamic marketplace is only going to leave behind those who don't adapt to it, while those who do adapt, are going to keep flourishing.

Continuous learning and developing skills are crucial because:

You Need to Adapt to External Changes

As you know, virtual sales are influenced by the heavy use of technology and other tools. When you stay updated on the newest efficient tools to use, the platforms to leverage your sales, and so on, you are going to keep succeeding.

For example, everyone is worried about AI taking over their jobs. This is true to an extent. If you don't use AI and leverage its potential to become efficient and effective at your work, then someone else who's using AI is going to steal your job. That's the reality!

AI is an example of a technological change that if you fail to adapt to it, others will adapt and dominate the market. Therefore, staying updated with new tech and tools is necessary for continuous growth and success.

Current Sales Techniques May Not Work Everytime

There is a need to improve your sales techniques and tactics over time. What might work now, might not work tomorrow.

Our sales teams had great success using one type of prospecting technique to get instant responses and leads through LinkedIn and Facebook.

But after a few months, we noticed a decline in response rates and this is because the current market has adapted to such outreach techniques imposed by other salespeople.

Hence, we had to do something different. We adapted and learned a new outreach technique and started getting high response rates and leads, even better than before.

The lesson here is you may leverage one kind of negotiation tactic, outreach method, lead source, etc., and it may work brilliantly today, but you shouldn't be caught out when it doesn't work tomorrow.

Always look to keep improving your selling skills and have more tricks up your sleeves to overcome tough situations down the road.

Building Customer Relationships Is a Long-Term Game

Maintaining strong customer relationships is important for your business. But customers too adapt their behavior and choices over time.

If you stay behind new customer trends, and keep delivering what you used to work, they may look for another supplier. This is why keeping a constant communication line and feedback loop with the customer is crucial.

Actively listen to their feedback, changes in demands, and so on, to understand and respond to their requirements. As a result, you will foster loyalty.

Stay Ahead of Your Competitors

Lastly, you need to be open to learning and skill development because that's how you can outperform other competitors and dominate the market.

If you are someone who leverages new technological and marketing trends, you are going to be more effective and beat your competition by miles. Thus, enhancing your virtual sales results.

Let's now look into a few ways in which you can improve your skills. For me, I find these very effective:

Doing Online Courses and Getting Certifications

Online courses are a lot cheaper than you think and pretty convenient to do at your own pace.

Check out platforms like Udemy and Coursera to find sales and tech-related courses that you can learn and enhance your skills.

Even platforms like Google hold a free Skillshop where you can learn digital marketing and how to run paid ad campaigns with detailed tutorials. You would even get a certification in digital marketing from Google after completing the whole course.

Having a Mentor or Coach

Connecting with a mentor or a coach online is a great way to upskill yourself. In fact, it's the fastest and most efficient way to do so because you are going to learn the things that work and avoid learning irrelevant and redundant information like you would see on social media and blogs.

Compared to online courses, joining a mentorship program does cost more but it is definitely worth it to improve your skills over time and even learn advanced selling techniques.

Look for mentors and coaches who give you continuous feedback, are comfortable to work with, give proper guidance, and are heavily interested in supporting your professional growth.

Attending Workshops and Webinars

You don't need to attend workshops or seminars physically anymore, because you have online workshops and webinars.

Participate in workshops and webinars that are specific to your industry so that you can keep up with market trends and also learn new ways to connect and retain clients.

Reading and Absorbing Knowledge

Reading books, reports, research papers, articles, etc., can also help you acquire new information and pick up on advanced skills.

I enjoy reading books such as *The Challenger Sale* by Brent Adamson and Dixon Matthew and *Never Split the Difference* by Christopher Voss. I will cover a special selling technique in the next chapter based on the former book.

Instill a habit where you enjoy reading daily and you will see the changes when you pick up new valuable information and improve on your development (just like how you are doing right now with this book).

Practice Leads to More Success

Practice indeed makes one perfect! Keep practicing the new techniques you pick up and do role-playing sessions regularly with your colleagues or friends.

This helps you to put yourself in a real-life situation and improve on areas where you feel might need some work.

It is crucial to keep practicing to be efficient in handling objections and articulately delivering your pitch. This helps in improving your sales performance (make sure you do this virtually so you are an expert in that particular environment).

Staying Motivated and Avoiding Burnout in Remote Sales

We conclude this chapter by going through a reality check; It's not easy to maintain yourself as an effective virtual salesperson. Even if you are having months of immense success, hitting way above your sales targets, and maintaining happy relationships with customers, there will be rough patches along the journey.

This is where staying motivated and avoiding burnout is crucial. It can be easy to be burned out in remote sales because we get distracted by a lot of things in the virtual world and our minds can easily shift attention to other things.

To stay focused, motivated, and avoid burnout, here are some strategies that can help you:

Have Clarity on Goals and Set Priorities

Having well-defined goals helps remove uncertainty and give you a clear direction. This is why I suggest using the SMART goal-setting approach to help you with this.

When you are pursuing defined goals, you can head into each day with a solid plan and break down tasks into smaller manageable actions. This helps you set priorities for what needs to be done urgently, what can be automated, and what can be discarded. Protect your time and energy!

Establish a Routine with a Structure

A routine creates consistency, but this can result to positive or negative changes. A poor routine without structure leads to inefficiency in your work.

Therefore, you must create a structured routine that helps you turn up consistently and increase your virtual sales efforts.

You can do this by creating a consistent work schedule, creating time blocks for each specific task you do, and utilizing your energy on tasks that require more of your brain power first thing in the morning.

Moreover, your workspace and environment should encourage productivity. Remove distractions from your space and also ensure it creates boundaries between your personal life and work.

Treat Breaks as Divine Recharge Periods

Breaks are extremely important during your work time. I'm not suggesting doing some sort of Pomodoro technique and taking breaks. I'm suggesting to focus on the quality of your breaks rather than how many breaks you take.

When you take breaks, refrain from scrolling on social media for instance, as this won't let you switch off from your previous task that easily, and moreover, it still can drain your mental energy from constant scrolling.

It's better to go out and take a walk. This relaxes your mind and you would even do a little brainstorming that provides you with creative thoughts on how you can optimize your work performance.

Even doing some stretches, staying hydrated, and speaking to someone you care about in your breaks help you to stay active and motivated to continue where you left off.

Stay Socially Connected

The social element is crucial because nowadays you see hustle culture and ultra-productivity tactics encourage isolation. While isolation can help you get tons of work done, this is not a sustainable approach.

Isolation can lead to demotivation and sometimes depression. This is why it's important to stay connected with your team and other members of your social circle.

If within a team, schedule regular meetings to check in with their progress, provide updates, and also motivate each other to strive towards achieving a specific goal.

In the virtual setting, you can do many sorts of things. You can host informal meets such as a mini-coffee break, lunch break, and even creative meets like sharing one's pets or hobbies.

Keep Learning

Be open to constantly learning and improving yourself by taking online courses, reading books, webinars, and other ways mentioned in the previous section.

Working on your personal development makes you more confident and motivated to keep growing and fulfilling your goals.

Condition Yourself Daily

Lastly, look to take care of yourself by incorporating enough sleep, doing plenty of physical exercise, and maintaining a healthy diet.

Sounds basic but trust me, when you include these three pillars in your life, you will experience each day with energy and motivation. As a result, this will reflect on your work performance too.

As you stay motivated and avoid signs of burnout, remote selling becomes more of a meaningful vocation and you will stay focused on achieving any goals you set towards achieving.

Virtual Selling Prep Exercise: Set Your SMART Goals

In this exercise, you will use the lessons you have learned in this chapter and set **THREE** goals using the **SMART** method. These three goals should relate to:

1. Improving your current virtual sales process (This can be increasing your sales, lead response rates, implementing a new outreach or sales strategy to improve results, etc.)

2. Launching a new project (This can be exploring a new market segment and identifying selling opportunity, it can also relate to a side-hustle that you always wanted to do but didn't find the time to do so)

3. Learn a new skill (this can be something that can compliment your virtual sales skills such as digital marketing, public speaking, funnel hacking, mastering AI tools, etc. It can also be something you personally wanted to do such as learning a new instrument, coding, martial arts, and so on)

I'm giving you the space here to ponder and set your goals clear and specific according to the **SMART** way.

This gives you clarity on your goals and you don't get overwelmed by it because you are setting three goals that belong

> **to separate categories.**

We have discussed plenty on how you can optimize your virtual sales performance here, but do you want insights on some of the advanced virtual selling skills that you can use?

Then, the next chapter is going to reveal to you some tricks that I find effective which very much will interest you.

Chapter 7:

Advanced Virtual Sales Strategies

Ready to learn a few advanced virtual selling strategies?

In this chapter, I will cover three distinctive advanced selling techniques you can use for virtual selling:

1. Account-Based Selling (ABS)

2. Collaborative Selling

3. The "Challenger Sale" Approach

You will understand the foundations of each selling approach and how you can align it with selling your products or services.

As a bonus, I will share a few important negotiation tactics you can use for remotely sealing deals.

Let's get right into it and get to understand each advanced sales approach!

Account-Based Selling in the Virtual Landscape

First up, we have account-based selling, or ABS for short. How does this differ from the traditional way of prospecting?

Well, the traditional prospecting method involves trying to cast a wide net to attract many potential customers into your funnel. Then, you qualify interested buyers, nurture them, and eventually convert them.

On the other hand, account-based selling involves focusing on a specific account or a potential high-value customer and hyperpersonalizing your message to convert them.

In other words, you treat a specific company you are targeting as an entire market for you to target. You engage with the key decision-makers, and other stakeholders in that company in order to understand them better and eventually nurture the contacts into conversion.

The benefit of using ABS is that it is regarded as a *consultative* way of selling. This is because you will prioritize relationship-building with various key stakeholders within that account, and inquire about their pain points, thus, finding ways to provide value and strengthen the bond.

Simply put, you are like a consultant who is put on this planet to help them solve problems rather than being a direct salesman.

ABS is highly strategic when it comes to targeted outreach. You reach out to various contacts within that account and establish relationships and provide them with the urgency to work with you.

When it comes to productivity purposes, ABS gives you a clear direction on focusing your resources on one account and seeing the results for it, rather than putting less energy into various individual prospects and show no results for it.

Step-By-Step Guide for Conducting Account-Based Selling

Let's now look into how you can strategically conduct your ABS process. Simply follow these steps:

Step 1: Select Your Target Company

This will be an easy task once you properly know your ideal customer avatar or profile.

Is your target customer a Fortune 500 company or a SME? Do your marketing and sales efforts align with serving this type of company?

Take, for example, you might be selling ERP to manufacturing firms. You make a list of manufacturing companies in your market and choose the few that fit your ideal customer profile.

With a list of potential companies at your helm, you can prioritize and target companies that fit right into your ideal customer list.

Remember that when you use the ABS approach, you choose and focus your efforts on only a few accounts, don't take on more. Keep in mind that less is more.

Step 2- Identify Your Contacts Within Each Account

After selecting a target company as your account, you need to know which individuals belong to your purchasing group.

The best way to understand is to know who is going to use your product or service (users), who is going to manage these users (managers), and who all are going to have the final say in having this deal closed (key decision makers).

Continuing with our previous example, as you are targeting manufacturing companies, you will know that:

- The users that will use your ERP system are individuals in accounting, finance, administration, payroll, inventory, procurement, and production.

- The managers are those individuals who are managing the users in each department.

- Whereas, the key decision-makers could be the board, CFO, CTO, or CEO.

You can identify each of these individuals using virtual platforms. Use LinkedIn for instance and look up your target company. Go to the

People section and you will find a list of individuals with job titles that match your customer profile. Then, you can reach out and connect with these individuals.

Step 3: Implement Customized Messaging

Next up, you can deliver personalized messaging to key stakeholders within the account.

Ensure you reach out to as many as stakeholders you can connect with and look to provide value. Provide useful content, webinars, and whitepapers, and exhibit social proof with case studies and testimonials.

It's ideal to learn more about the target company through their social media pages, website, reports, etc. This helps you understand their goals and challenges better, bring that up in your customized messages or conversations, and introduce your solution as their savior.

Step 4: Measure Your Account Activity

Lastly, measure and optimize.

Understand how well your account's activity is likely to be converted. Is there positive feedback on response rates? Are they engaging with you frequently and finding value from your contribution? Are they opening up to you and sharing their challenges?

You can score your accounts based on the above activity (and other indicators you may have) to make sure you can align your sales and marketing efforts to nurture them further and look to have the big talk! in sealing the deal.

Based on the score, you can understand how likely they are going to convert.

The ABS method might look as if you are going to spend some time to win the hearts of the customer, but it's a worthwhile strategy.

Relationship-building is key and especially when you have various stakeholders on your side, it gets better. You are more likely to retain such customers when you do end up converting them because you established strong bonds with various individuals within that account.

ABS is more of a long-term strategy that you can use to build foundations by researching in-depth about the company and establishing trust before closing them. Moreover, it aids in building long-term relationships with clients and retaining them for longer periods.

Collaborative Selling: Partnering with Clients Remotely

Let's now learn more about collaborative selling.

This approach prioritizes working with clients intimately to understand their needs, make them aware of their problems, and create solutions together.

In this case, collaborative selling means that you are seeing your prospect or client as a partner and you continually participate in problem-solving processes with them.

Think of how a doctor is in a well-respected position to sell you a prescription. Do you see doctors writing you a prescription first and then doing a diagnosis? Of course, not! That would be considered as a malpractice.

Likewise, in sales, if you decide to sell your products or services without diagnosing the prospect's business and actively seeking out what their problems are, then the prospect knows they are being sold something. They will show more resistance and end up disengaging with you.

No one likes to be sold something; instead, they like to buy. Keep this in mind. Therefore, your role is to be a partner to them, collaborate with them on identifying their problems as opportunities, and tailor your solution to fix them.

To summarize, the key characteristics of collaborative selling include:

- Being client-centric and focusing on the client's needs and addressing them.

- Viewing clients as partners and involving in the decision-making process.

- Involving in co-creation by collaboratively developing solutions with the client to solve problems.

Equipping Yourself to Be a Great Collaborative Business Partner

Here are a few ways in which you can successfully conduct collaborative selling remotely:

Have Polished Communication Channels

When you view your client as a partner, this means clear effective communication is key. Hence, utilize communication channels that help you to stay in touch and communicate freely with your prospects and clients.

Use tools like Zoom and Microsoft Teams for regular virtual meetings. Use Slack as a base communication platform to collaborate with their team and also include your team for various projects.

Utilize whiteboard tools and other graphical representational tools to conduct brainstorming sessions and communicate your and their ideas to make solutions together.

Be Analytical in Your Partnership

As you are partnering with your client, you need to be analytic and conduct an in-depth diagnosis of the client's business needs, goals, challenges, and pain points.

Keep meeting up virtually with the client and ask questions that help you gain insight. Conduct interviews and online surveys to understand and dig up information more effectively.

You can also utilize your CRM system analytics to understand your client's behavior and requirements.

Formulate Solutions Together

As mentioned earlier, co-creating solutions with your client is a big aspect of collaborative selling. This means you can organize several brainstorming sessions virtually with your client and formulate solutions together.

Utilize design tools such as Figma or Adobe to create prototypes of your ideas and how you want to implement them into your client's business.

This gives them clarity of what you bring to the table, helps you gain real-time feedback and input from the clients, and also makes you stand out from others.

Implement Solutions and Iterate Continuously

When you implement the solution, you should ensure the entire process goes smoothly.

You are building a solid long-term relationship with your client here so the last thing you would want is to bring them more inconveniences after they put their faith in working with you.

This is why it is crucial to work closely with your clients during the implementation phase and most tech companies idolize this ritual.

Not only do you need to ensure your solution meets your client's expectations, but also you need to keep communicating with them to gather feedback on the solution.

This helps you to identify how you can improve the solution and make necessary fixes here and there to improve your solution over time.

Iteration comes after when you implement a minimal viable product (MVP). Hence, don't look to go out guns blazing and deliver your best solution upfront.

Don't strive for perfection. Yes, first impressions are important but you should introduce a solution where you believe improvements are possible over time.

This gives you the leeway to keep iterating and improving your solution for your client in the long term. They will be thankful for it and you will retain them for years.

Let's understand this better using the example we used in the previous section—offering ERP solutions to manufacturing companies.

You look to conduct your research by gathering information on your target manufacturing company. You get their CFO or CTO to book a discovery call with you and you get to know about their processes, whether they are already using an ERP or multiple software, and also their current pain points.

Based on the call, you can then look to customize your proposal to tailor your ERP solution to address each pain point you have dug up about the manufacturing company.

In the virtual meet, you can organize a collaborative workshop with the manufacturing company where you showcase your proposal and demonstrate using prototypes and charts on how your ERP solution will meet their expectations.

You then educate them on the implementation process and how the departmental teams of your company will work with them closely during this phase.

You would provide training for users during the implementation phase so that they get equipped to use your ERP solution and have no trouble with it. You also allow them to share insights and you can gain feedback to make adjustments along the way.

A better way you can do this is to launch a pilot program where you implement the ERP system on a smaller scale in the manufacturing company. You can then allow users in that company to report feedback to you every couple of times a week so you can address issues and refine your ERP solution.

In addition, you provide training at the same time through online module content you may have prepared, live sessions, and also send them user manuals virtually. Eventually, you can smoothly transition into a full-scale implementation of the ERP.

You ensure there will be continuous support for the manufacturing company and hold regular virtual meetings with them to discuss areas for improvement.

As you can see, you are approaching this with a sense of partnership rather than just treating them as a transactional client. You want to build a good relationship with them and keep working with them. It's more than just transactions to you.

Collaborative selling may seem more client-centric but it doesn't limit you to make use of the team you have. And this is not your sales team alone. I'm talking about your marketing team, IT team, product team, finance team, etc.

It's collaborative after all and when you include your company departments into the mix and get them to work closely with the prospect, you see amazing results.

The "Challenger Sale" Approach in Virtual Selling

Let's talk about the "Challenger Sale" methodology now. This concept was inspired from the book *The Challenger Sale* by Adamson and Dixon.

According to the book, a Challenger sales rep is considered to be someone who offers a different perspective to the customer's world, understands their business, teaches them things they don't know and is not afraid to push the customer out of their comfort zone.

In a nutshell, when you adopt the Challenger Sale approach, you must account for these three specific traits:

- Provide unique insights into the conversation by teaching the customer something new that they haven't noticed before and impress them with your highly intelligent skills.

- Reframe and customize your sales conversation to address the customer's specific requirements and pain points.

- Confidently take control of the sale by challenging the customer's way of thinking and overcoming objections with assertiveness.

When you adopt this way of selling, the biggest advantage here is that you can stand out from other providers. This is because you are coming with a unique perspective that other salespeople don't. Moreover, you will focus your energy on understanding what drives the customer and also open talks to budget smoothly.

However, it must be said that this approach usually works best for high-performing sales reps who have a lot of experience in their field. If sales reps are used to the relationship-building style of selling, it can be challenging to adopt this approach. But it doesn't mean it's impossible to adopt it, just that it will take some training to do so.

The Challenger Sale approach is well-suited for sales processes which are often complex (such as selling software and other complex products/services) and shouldn't be used for selling solutions that solve simple problems (like selling apparel through e-commerce, etc.).

Step-By-Step Guide to Become a "Challenger"

Let's now look at how you can implement this approach in real life. The Challenger Sale approach typically takes your customer on an emotional rollercoaster ride.

There will be times in a conversation when you get them excited and also get them into an emotional state. But then you bring back that excitement by introducing your solution.

Here are the steps to make it clear:

Stage 1: Warm Up

The first engagement with your customer should be to establish credibility and authority from the get-go.

So, express your knowledge and intelligence in this phase by showing how well you know the subject and also educate them on something they don't know.

One shouldn't underestimate the customer's intelligence, however. Most customers are well-educated on what they are seeking, they are just rather confused on which provider they should choose from a list of endless good options.

As you know, most can access information instantly using the internet and get sufficient knowledge.

Hence, do approach this stage with a little caution and don't be a Mr. "Know-It-All." Instead, be someone who offers a unique perspective and facts that pique the customer's curiosity levels.

Get creative by using interactive content and tools that you can engage virtually with the prospect and show how educated you are in your particular field.

And it must be said, don't bring up your solution at all at this stage. We're only warming up!

Stage 2: Reframe

During the prospect conversation, not only you will reveal your knowledge, but it also open up the customer to share their challenges.

By this stage, you will gain insights into many of the prospect's problems. This is where you hit the Reframe button. Switch the conversation by bringing a new perspective that they never thought of.

Reframing the conversation requires you to stay on topic, address the customer's limiting beliefs, and also address their problem from an interesting perspective.

For example, if you are selling ERP and your customer's specific pain point they brought up is not generating more revenue due to high lead time and lack of inefficency in their business, then you can reframe by saying:

This is quite a common issue and it is mostly due to not having the systems integrated in one place. Did you know many companies integrate everything in one system and this saves X hours per week and generates five times the revenue? It isn't the problem with your business, just a simple productivity fix.

Just like that you can change the perspective of the customer's mind and remove any limiting beliefs they had that bring resistance to your conversation.

You can also back up your claims by providing more facts, case studies, and interactive content.

Stage 3: Elevate Emotions

In this phase, you make the conversation emotional by tapping more into the prospect's heart.

You can do this by a little storytelling, sharing client success stories that they can relate to, and bringing new perspectives from your research.

Your goal is to instill desire into the customer's mind so that they feel determined to address and fix the problem urgently.

Stage 4: Value proposition

In this phase, you look to bring their hopes up by painting a better future for them. Tell them not everything is going to be doom and gloom and this is where you take control of the sale.

And yes, you still haven't introduced your product or service yet. Instead, you give them an idea of how positive their future would look like with your solution.

Provide more stories of businesses that implemented the same solution and got tangible results to show for. Make them understand the result they will get and how that solution is going to be the one that bridges that gap.

Stage 5: Make the Offer

Finally, after getting their hopes up high and painting a new future with that solution you shared, it's time to bring your product or service into the conversation.

Show them that you have the solution at your fingertips and they are only a few minutes away from getting access to it (Well, it depends on the nature of the product or service you are selling but you get my point!).

That's the Challenger Sale approach for you and another advanced strategy that you can use with your virtual sales process.

One huge disclaimer before wrapping up this section!

Use all these advanced selling strategies ONLY after establishing your virtual sales processes and ensuring they run smoothly.

Use the lessons in Chapter 2 and build your robust virtual sales process so that you get the basics right.

Only then, you can implement advanced strategies by leveraging your virtual infrastructure and sealing deals remotely.

Negotiation Tactics for Closing High-Stakes Deals Virtually

We will wrap up this chapter by discussing a few negotiation tactics you could use for closing deals virtually.

Just like traditional selling, these tactics will work effectively. The only difference is you have to tailor your message clearly and deliver the solution virtually.

I won't make this big but here are a few tactics that I recommend you use in your virtual sales process:

The Puppy Dog Close

This negotiation tactic was inspired by pet store owners allowing the customer to take a puppy dog to their home for a limited time at no cost.

They could choose to return it after the time runs out, but in most cases, they never did and end up paying for the puppy. This tactic works because pet store owners know customers will eventually develop an emotional connection with the pet.

Allowing to take the puppy home for free (like a free trial period) was just to lower selling resistance.

Likewise, you can use the puppy dog close to whatever you are selling virtually. If you are selling software, offer a free trial for a couple of weeks. Then, if the customer loves it, they can choose to pay the subscription.

If you are selling services such as a sales training program, you can agree to a trial period where you deliver the service for a couple of weeks and if they don't get any tangible results, they don't need to pay.

This helps you to influence the buyer so that they show little to no resistance to committing to your offer.

The Risk Reversal

The whole point of a risk reversal is to remove any risk from the buyer so that they feel more confident to buying your offer.

Hence, it is important to identify key areas in your offer where you can implement risk reversal so that the customer doesn't show more resistance to accepting your product or services.

A common risk reversal technique is to include guarantees especially in the form of money-back guarantees. Simply include a guarantee that if your product or service doesn't satisfy your customers, they have the right to get a full refund.

Of course, include terms and conditions in your guarantee so that you can avoid unethical customers taking advantage of your guarantee. For example, conditions can provide evidence of why they aren't satisfied and facts and figures to show they didn't receive the results they expected from your product or service.

This helps to make your gaurantees more clear and the buyer to eventually agree to your terms.

Create Urgency and Scarcity

Probably one of the oldest tricks in the book, but works for a reason! Simply create urgency and scarcity in your offers so it allows buyers to take action quickly.

In your sales calls, you can suggest that you have limited slots or products available, so they have to decide quickly. Or for your sales pages and emails, you can tell them there's a discount they can take advantage of but it can be only availed by the end of the month.

This helps create urgency within buyers and initiate FOMO (fear of missing out) syndrome, hence you can close deals quickly this way.

Bring on Social Proof

Social proof always works! Leverage your social proof by showcasing case studies, testimonials, and success stories in your virtual presentations and sales pages.

I don't need to go into much detail about this as you already know the power of social proof from the earlier chapters.

Bonuses

Bonuses are add-ons you include in your offers to make the customers believe they are getting more out of the deal than what they are paying.

This helps make your offers more appealing. For example, if you are selling software, you can add bonuses such as another software or hardware shipped for free, and some modules of training the users and warranty also for free.

Prince Anchoring

This is one of my favorite negotiation tactics and I use it during a live call and also on sales pages. The thing is you set an initial price as a point where the customer can refer to, it and make them believe they are going to commit to that price.

But later on in your sales call or sales page, you present the actual price of your product or service which is in the form of a special discount for a limited time.

Some salespeople take this further by adding additional price anchors. For example, you can introduce the initial price of a program to be $7,999 and tell them this is what your program is worth in value.

Then, you can present what you are going to sell the program for and this would be an affordable $3,999 from the initial price. For the icing on the cake, you introduce that there's a special discount available at only $1,999 for a limited time.

This makes your offer too irresistible to turn down.

Multiple Buying Options

You see many software companies do this and that is offering multiple offers to users in the form of subscription plans or packages.

This works for a reason because buyers can compare the value they get from different plans and classify them based on tiers. This allows them to choose the best package for their needs.

Hence, wherever possible, offer at least three different plans and packages to your prospect so that they get enticed by options and eventually pick one that suits their needs and budget.

When you include the above negotiation tactics in your live virtual meetings and virtual sales processes, you are going to see amazing results.

Remember that it is essential that your product or service does meet up to the expectations, however. False claims and marketing must be avoided and you should be ethical when making irresistible offers.

Virtual Selling Prep Exercise: It's Okay to Be Judged!

> This is the final exercise for you. Being judged is something that a virtual salesperson can take as a positive feedback cycle rather than a negative one.
>
> Your task is to find someone, a friend or a family, who will watch, listen, or read your sales conversation with a prospect. Then, they will provide you feedback on where they think you could improve.
>
> This exercise is basically an ego-busting one. It might not be comfortable to have someone you know to nod their head into your conversation with a prospect, and somewhat judge your style.
>
> But this brings you out of your comfort zone, and confident of having a sales conversation in front of anyone. By the end of the day, you need to ensure you engage with prospects and meet their expectations.
>
> The person you choose for this exercise can be optional. I would usually suggest picking someone you know who would be a salesperson themselves. This makes the exercise even more insightful for you.
>
> And remember: It's okay to be judged. Take in the positives! You will ace this!

That wraps up the chapter!

You have learned three advanced selling approaches that you can use in your virtual sales process, plus a few exciting negotiation tactics that you can implement to close deals effectively.

What's next in store? You are equipped with the tools and knowledge to take your virtual sales journey to another level.

But before that, let's understand how you should be in it for the long run.

Let's explore the future of virtual sales.

Chapter 8:

Adapting to the Future of Virtual Sales

As I mentioned when you started to read this book, virtual selling is here to stay and it's for the future. You must only take this profession seriously if you are only in it for the long run.

This is why it is important to be aware of the future of virtual sales and adapt to it.

This short chapter will give you a brief overview of what you can expect in the future when it comes to virtual selling and how you can embrace the dynamic world of virtual sales.

Let's explore the emerging trends for starters!

Emerging Trends in Remote Selling

Virtual selling has a great future in store because of emerging trends.

Many of these trends are simply a recap of what you have learned throughout the book but a sign that virtual sales teams should invest in these areas heavily for a seamless future.

Here is a list of emerging trends that you should keep in mind:

Sales Automation

For making sales operations run smoothly and scalable, the need for automation has become necessary.

Automation reduces the risk of human errors and allows sales teams to scale efficiently.

In what ways is this particular trend emerging?

Firstly, the rise of AI and machine learning enters the conversation. Virtual sales teams are integrating AI into their processes, making their workflow efficient and more effective.

This allows them to spare room and resources to focus on other aspects that require better human intervention.

And secondly, automation tools as we have learned: CRM systems, email marketing automation, social media engagement platforms, etc., to maximize productivity and reduce the burden of manual repetitive tasks.

Data-Driven Decision-Making

Data has become too crucial for virtual sales teams to leverage and close deals remotely.

For instance, leveraging data analytics helps teams to understand more about their prospect's behavior and optimize their sales strategy.

Also, predictive analysis helps teams to predict selling trends and evaluate customer needs. Furthermore, data helps bring insights from customer interactions and allow teams to personalize their sales messages accurately.

Social Selling

As we learned in detail in the earlier chapters, social selling is not only a modern-day approach but also a trend that looks to solidify the future of virtual sales.

I simply can't think that in a few years the number of social media users would significantly decrease. Can you?

You are neither early nor late on jumping on a trend like social selling. It's here to stay and when you leverage social media channels to build relationships and engage with prospects, you are going to see effective results.

Establish yourself in multiple social media platforms, namely LinkedIn, Twitter, Facebook, and Instagram. Look out for platforms that will rise in the future and you can even target your customers there.

Moreover, build a content marketing system where you share valuable content, mainly on platforms such as YouTube and TikTok, leveraging its algorithm and having your content put in front of your ideal target customers.

Integrating Remote Collaboration Tools and Tech

I won't deny that in a few years, there will be a lot of remote tools to choose from. You are going to see some amazing and creative tools come out of nowhere and revolutionize how you conduct your virtual selling.

You can currently leverage platforms and tools like Zoom, Google Meet, Slack, Trello, etc. now, and still easily transition your virtual sales process to new tools that may provide you better results in the future.

Integrating these remote collaboration tools into your virtual sales process is easy. Moreover, integrating systems such as CRMs and ERP can be the backbone of your virtual sales operations.

Incorporating an E-Commerce Environment

As more people find it convenient to purchase things online, it is important to integrate your virtual sales process into an e-commerce-like environment.

This means preparing your websites, landing pages, etc., as a digital store so that customers can easily whip out their credit card and buy after getting enticed by your offers.

Make your central hub of sales (your website) accessible and convenient for customers, with multiple payment options so you don't miss out on that crucial sale. It is your way to visually present your solution and urge them to buy.

Preparing for the Evolution of Virtual Sales Technology

Adapting to the future of virtual sales is all about preparation. How meticulously you think about the future influences your decision at the present.

Here are a few ways one can prepare for the evolution of virtual sales technology:

Invest in Advanced Tools

Investing in the right tools helps you to be ready for the future. For example, ensure you invest in a CRM system that is scalable and can easily integrate with the latest tech.

Dive deep into AI and machine learning-driven tools that can maximize your productivity and automate repetitive tasks.

Keep Learning

You should instill a growth mindset by continuously learning and seeking to be better. This helps you to identify new ways to leverage technology and also identify tools that help to improve your virtual sales process.

The best way to maintain a learning habit is by taking up training programs to use new tools and advanced tech and keeping up with your industry to be aware of new trends and innovations.

Upgrade Your Virtual Infrastructure

Having a robust IT infrastructure can ensure your virtual sales process runs smoothly for decades.

When I mean by IT infrastructure, I'm talking about everything that's associated with it: your internet connection, servers, software, and hardware you use.

Invest in high-quality internet connection, secure servers, and reliable software and hardware.

Moreover, consider cybersecurity as a top priority and look to implement measures to safeguard sensitive data such as customer information, trade secrets, etc., and conduct regular security audits to protect your infrastructure.

Thriving in a Hybrid Sales Environment

A hybrid sales environment means working in a sales environment where you combine remote selling and also in-person interactions. It's utilizing the best of both worlds.

Let's understand how you can thrive in a hybrid sales environment:

Find the Right Balance

If you want to dominate in a hybrid selling environment, the number one effective trait you could possess is being flexible.

Your ability to understand your prospects' and customers' comfort zones and what they prefer to use for interactions is crucial.

You may have some clients who are comfortable with remote interactions for complex deals while some prefer having in-person meetings.

Therefore, you need to adapt to these conditions and ensure the collaboration goes smoothly.

It's All About Communicating Effectively

Whether it is in-person interactions or virtual collaboration, ensure your communication lines are clear, crisp, and tailored effectively to your customer.

You can leverage interactive components in virtual settings such as Q&A sessions, webinars, live demos, polls, etc., to increase engagement. Whereas, you can conduct physical workshops, seminars, and in-person consultation sessions to build rapport as well.

Unify Your Sales Process

It is important to integrate both your in-person sales strategy and virtual sales strategy. For example, ensure your CRM systems track both types of interactions and store data to facilitate a seamless customer journey experience.

Diversify Your Toolbox

To dominate a hybrid selling environment, you need to be equipped with tools to cater to both worlds.

This is why you should establish a diversified toolbox so when you have situations where clients don't have access to Zoom for instance, you can either adopt other video conferencing tools, emails, or even a simple phone call.

Most efficient salespeople leverage multiple tools over time. From sending short video DMs to prospects to inviting them over to their place for a cup of coffee, it is important to have multiple tricks up your sleeves and not become one-dimensional with your approach.

Embracing Change and Innovation in Virtual Sales

We will wrap up this chapter by understanding how you can embrace change in virtual sales.

It can be executed by:

Fostering an Innovative Culture

Encourage experimenting with new strategies and tools in your virtual sales operations.

When you are not afraid to try new things and do it in a diligent way (without affecting your current workflow), you can identify new opportunities to leverage and maximize your sales output.

Moreover, if you are managing a team, encourage everyone to provide innovative ideas and reward them for implementing new effective strategies.

Maintaining a Customer-Centric Approach

I still believe the customer-centric approach will not fade away in the next few years and anyone working in sales is going to maximize their results when they adopt this approach.

Maintain constant feedback loops with your customers to keep understanding their needs and pain points. Embrace this as identifying new opportunities to provide more value and retain them.

Moreover, the customer-centric approach is as personalized as it gets! You can leverage technology and tools at your helm to tailor your solution to address specific customer requirements.

Being Agile

Based on the agile methodology in project management, being agile in simple words means adapting to changes in the market quickly so that you keep maximizing your output over time.

Therefore, embrace a solid mindset of continuously looking to improve and refine your virtual sales strategies and adapt quickly to dynamic market trends.

When you spend too much time, pondering decisions, and over-evaluating emerging trends, you could be left behind by your competition and the market itself.

So, be agile and keep dominating!

When you follow the above mindset and embrace change, you will find it easy to adapt to changes in the market.

The future of virtual sales is in good hands and it is your role to stay in it for the long run and maximize your selling potential.

Leverage this time and achieve your goals!

Conclusion:

Putting Your Virtual Sales Skills into Action

You have reached the end of this educational journey and are maximizing your knowledge of virtual sales.

You have equipped yourself with a collection of strategies, practical tips, and insights that you can now implement to transform your way of selling.

Virtual selling is a permanently ingrained skill. You keep polishing it by surrounding yourself with innovative remote tools and technology that help you stay efficient and produce results.

Let's recap what you have learned:

- Introduction to virtual sales: Trends and statistics to back up its rise, the advantages and challenges of virtual selling, and the essential skills you need to succeed in this field.

- The virtual sales process: How prospecting looks like in the digital age, the "LASER" method for identifying high-quality leads, leveraging email outreach, the art of social selling, navigating the virtual sales funnel, and the "CLOSE" framework for sealing important deals remotely.

- Building relationships virtually: How to establish trust and rapport online, the significance of active listening, how you can confidently overcome objections and concerns, and how to nurture long-term client relationships virtually.

- Leveraging technology for virtual sales: Knowing the essential tools you need for remote selling, how to master video sales calls, the importance of integrating CRM in virtual sales, and automation strategies for streamlining your process.

- Targeting technical niches: Understanding the technical buyer's mindset, how to identify lucrative technical niches with examples, how you can tailor your sales message, and also become a credible advisor in technical sales.

- Optimizing your performance: How to set goals, measure and analyze your virtual sales performance, and the importance of adopting a growth mindset and staying motivated to avoid burnout.

- Advanced strategies: Understanding strategies such as account-based selling, collaborative selling, the "challenger sale" approach, and a few negotiation tactics to help close high-stakes deals.

- Adapting to the future: Understanding the emerging trends in remote selling, preparing for the evolution of virtual sales technology, dominating in a hybrid selling environment, and embracing change.

Virtual sales represent how we connect, engage, and do business with people. It is the present and future!

From learning the beauty of a virtual sales funnel to the significance of social selling, your role is to leverage tools and technology and make your life easier to sell your solution to customers.

But the knowledge alone here isn't enough! Take action! Now is the time to do so. I urge you to start by implementing the mini exercises that you have read in each chapter and start building confidence and experience in the world of virtual selling.

And most importantly, enjoy the process! I've been in sales for years and leveraged virtual selling because I enjoy what I do. It's a passion that no one can take away from me and you should feel the same when you want to succeed in this field.

Start your virtual selling journey or optimize your current journey with the knowledge and tools you have acquired.

To your virtual selling success,

Kelli Stello

Appendices

Virtual Sales Success Stories

Small business like Slate & Tell, Momentary Ink, Princess Polly, BM Collagen, Tzuki, and Genify Studio improved their digital success by crafting their viral TikTok marketing strategy. Read their stories here: https://blog.wishpond.com/post/115675438226/small-business-tiktok

Focusing on personalization strategies helped Heathrow Airport boost their digital revenue by 30%. Read the full story here: https://www.salesforce.com/resources/customer-stories/heathrow-personalisation-digital-revenue/

How leveraging data and centralizing it improved Make-A-Wish Foundation's collaboration and granted more wishes to children. Read the full story here: https://www.salesforce.com/resources/customer-stories/make-a-wish-data-changes-lives/

bp agents leveraged AI chat tool to save almost 4,000 hours. Read the full story here: https://www.salesforce.com/customer-stories/bp/

Marlie Andersch's remote data services company rockITdata, saw amazing growth by utilizing SBA pandemic programs and highlighting the importance of adapting to remote work conditions. Read the full story here: https://www.sba.gov/success-story/rockitdata-shoots-success-sbas-pandemic-programs

Pavel Stepanov's Virtudesk, a virtual assistant service, helped thousands of business owners to grow and become a major success. Read the full story here: https://medium.com/authority-magazine/pavel-stepanov-of-virtudesk-i-am-living-proof-of-the-american-dream-7761bd1874a5

Remote Selling Resources and Tools

Communication and Video Conferencing Tools

1. Zoom
2. Microsoft Teams
3. Google Meet
4. Skype
5. Cisco Webex
6. Loom
7. Demodesk
8. Dubb
9. Twist

Customer Relationship Management (CRM) Systems

1. Salesforce
2. HubSpot
3. Zoho CRM
4. Close
5. FiveCRM

6. Pipedrive
7. SalesTable
8. Freshsales

Sales Engagement Platforms

1. Outreach
2. SalesLoft
3. Groove
4. Yesware
5. Mailshake
6. Apollo.io
7. Reply
8. Mixmax
9. Drift

E-Signature Tools

1. DocuSign
2. Adobe Sign
3. HelloSign
4. PandaDoc
5. SignNow
6. SignRequest

7. OneSpan Sign

8. Signeasy

Marketing Automation Tools

1. Marketo
2. ActiveCampaign
3. Mailchimp
4. ConverKit
5. Klaviyo
6. HubSpot Marketing Hub
7. SendinBlue
8. Pardot
9. Drip
10. Autopilot

Prospecting and Lead Generation Tools

1. LinkedIn Sales Navigator
2. ZoomInfo
3. Clearbit
4. Hunter
5. LeadFuze
6. Clearbit

7. Leadfeeder

8. BuiltWith

9. Profiler

Analytics and Reporting Tools

1. Google Analytics

2. Tableau

3. InsightSquared

4. Clari

5. Gong

6. Mixpanel

7. timetoreply

8. Looker

9. Chorus

10. Geckoboard

Collaboration and Project Management Tools

1. Trello

2. Asana

3. Toggl

4. Basecamp

5. Monday.com

6. Harvest
7. Apploye Time Tracker
8. Notion

Customer Support Tools

1. Zendesk
2. Freshdesk
3. Intercom
4. LiveChat
5. Help Scout
6. Zoho Desk
7. Kayako
8. Front
9. Hiver
10. HelpDesk

Social Selling Tools

1. Hootsuite
2. Buffer
3. Sprout Social
4. SocialBee
5. Post Planner

6. TweetDeck
7. BuzzSumo
8. Sendible
9. CoSchedule
10. Falcon.io

Additional Tools That Will Come in Handy

1. Calendly
2. Google Workspace
3. Grammarly
4. Dropbox
5. Canva
6. Miro
7. Content Harmony
8. Wordpress
9. Vidyard
10. Podio
11. Seidat
12. Tandem
13. Limecall

Webinars

1. **HubSpot Webinars:** https://www.hubspot.com/webinars
2. **Salesforce Webinars:** https://www.salesforce.com/form/events/webinars/
3. **LinkedIn Sales Solutions Webinars:** https://business.linkedin.com/sales-solutions/webinars

Online Forums

1. **Reddit - r/Sales:** https://www.reddit.com/r/sales/
2. **Quora:** https://www.quora.com/
3. **GrowthHackers:** https://growthhackers.com/

Online Courses and Certifications

1. **HubSpot Academy:** https://academy.hubspot.com/
2. **Coursera:** https://www.coursera.org/
3. **LinkedIn Learning:** https://www.linkedin.com/learning/
4. **Udemy:** https://www.udemy.com/

Blogs

1. **Salesforce Blog:** https://www.salesforce.com/blog/
2. **HubSpot Sales Blog:** https://blog.hubspot.com/sales
3. **Gartner Blog:** https://www.gartner.com/en/insights

Podcasts

1. The Advanced Selling Podcast (Available on Apple Podcasts and Spotify)

2. Sales Gravy Podcast by Jeb Blount (Available on Spotify)

3. Make It Happen Mondays by John Barrows (Available on Apple Podcasts and Spotify)

Virtual Sales Glossary

Account-Based Selling (ABS): A strategy that focuses on closing high-value accounts by conducting personalized outreach and tailored offers.

AI (Artificial Intelligence): The ability of machines to adopt human intelligence and execute intellectual tasks such as learning, problem-solving, and reasoning.

Analytics: Systematic analysis using data or statistics to gain a flow of insights and get informed for better decision-making.

B2B (Business-to-Business): Typically, sales transactions done between two or more businesses, and not involving individual consumers.

B2C (Business-to-Consumer): Typically, sales transactions done between a business and individual consumers.

Buyer Persona: An almost fictional representation or profile of an ideal customer, formed from existing data about customers and market research.

CRM (Customer Relationship Management): Technology used for storing and managing a business's interactions and relationships with existing customers and prospects.

Cold Calling: Act of reaching out to potential prospects who have not previously come in contact or expressed interest in the business's product or service.

Conversion Rate: Accounts for the percentage of prospects who have took the desired action such as purchasing or signing up for a product or service.

Digital Sales Funnel: Refers to the online version of the traditional sales funnel and represents each phase a customer goes through from awareness to purchase.

Discovery Call: An initial call with a prospect to learn about their needs, challenges, and goals to ensure the solution aligns to meet their requirements.

Down-selling: An act of encouraging customers to purchase a comparatively cheaper offer after not purchasing the initial expensive offer.

E-commerce: Refers to buying and selling of goods or services online.

Email Automation: Using software to send automated emails to various market segments based on triggers or content schedules.

Engagement Rate: Refers to the particular metric that measures the level of interaction with your content (usually social media content).

Follow-Up: The act of subsequently communicating with a prospect or customer after an initial interaction.

Freemium: A business model where basic services are offered for free and more advanced services can be charged.

Gamification: Incorporating game-design components and principles in non-game contexts, usually done to engage users and solve their needs.

Google Analytics: Web analytics service offered by Google to track and report website traffic and other insights.

Hybrid Sales Environment: A sales approach that combines a mix of virtual and face-to-face interactions.

Inbound Marketing: Marketing strategy that attracts customers to one's business through useful and insightful content and lead magnets.

Inside Sales: Refers to sales performed remotely through phone, email, or online rather than utilizing in-person meetings.

Journey Mapping: A technique to visualize and comprehend the customer's experience from their point of view.

Key Performance Indicators (KPIs): Metrics used to measure the effectiveness of a sales process and whether it aligns to meet business and marketing goals.

Lead Generation: Refers to the process of identifying and capturing potential customers for a business.

Lead Nurturing: The process of developing relationships with prospects at various phases of the sales funnel or buying journey.

Marketing Automation: Utilizing technology to streamline marketing processes and campaigns across multiple channels.

Market Segmentation: Dividing a broad consumer or business market into sub-groups of consumers, usually done based on evaluating the type of shared characteristics.

Net Promoter Score (NPS): Refers to a particular metric used to evaluate customer loyalty and customer satisfaction.

Nurture Campaign: Series of communications established to engage and build relationships with leads through consistent, personalized messages.

Outbound Sales: Sales initiated through activities such as cold calling, email outreach, and social selling.

Opportunity: Refers to a qualified prospect in the sales pipeline that has the potential to become a customer.

Prospecting: The process of identifying potential buyers who may be interested in your offers.

Pipeline: Visual representation of a sales process to help sales teams manage their sales activities and close deals.

Qualifying: The act of determining whether a prospect has the potential or not to become a paying customer or buyer.

Quota: Refers to a sales target established for a salesperson or sales team to attain.

ROI (Return on Investment): Measures the profitability of an investment, usually calculated as the ratio of the net profit to the total investment cost.

Referral: New customer acquired through a recommendation from an existing customer.

Sales Enablement: Providing the sales team or business with the information, content, and tools to sell effectively.

Target Market: Refers to a specific group of potential customers that a business targets to sell their product or service.

Touchpoint: Any point of interaction between a business and a customer throughout the customer journey.

Upselling: The act of encouraging customers to purchase a more expensive offer or an upgrade to support their initial purchase.

User Experience (UX): Refers to the overall experience a user experiences while interacting with a product, service, or website.

Value Proposition: A statement that articulates how a product or service uniquely solves a problem or improves the situation for the customer.

Virtual Sales: Refers to the process of selling products or services remotely, focusing on using digital communication and remote tools.

Webinar: A seminar conducted online and allows for interactive elements and real-time feedback.

White Paper: An authoritative guide or report that provides detailed information on a specific topic, usually to help readers understand an issue or to solve it.

Zero Moment of Truth (ZMOT): Accounts for the moment in the buying journey when the consumer research about the product before the seller even knows that they exist.

References

Account-Based Selling - What Is It & How To Execute It? (2023, August 31). Klenty Blog. https://www.klenty.com/blog/what-is-account-based-selling/

Active Listening in Sales: The Ultimate Guide. (2023, January 2). HubSpot Blog. https://blog.hubspot.com/sales/active-listening-guide

Ahmed, E. (n.d.). *Virtual Selling: How to Build Relationships and Close Deals in the Age of Zoom.* LinkedIn. https://www.linkedin.com/pulse/virtual-selling-how-build-relationships-close-deals-age-eman-ahmed/

Airaghi, C. (2023, September 5). *The Best 6 Lead Scoring Criteria You Need | 2023 Update.* Breadcrumbs.io. https://breadcrumbs.io/blog/5-tried-tested-lead-scoring-criteria-2021/

Anderson, M. (n.d.). *What is Virtual Selling? (Definition, Examples, and Tips).* Www.impactplus.com. https://www.impactplus.com/blog/what-is-virtual-selling

Chevalier, S. (2024, February 6). *Global retail e-commerce sales 2014-2027.* Statista. https://www.statista.com/statistics/379046/worldwide-retail-e-commerce-sales/

Colas, C. V. (2021, March 25). *Pavel Stepanov of Virtudesk: I Am Living Proof Of The American Dream.* Authority Magazine. https://medium.com/authority-magazine/pavel-stepanov-of-virtudesk-i-am-living-proof-of-the-american-dream-7761bd1874a5

Collaborative Selling: How successful B2B companies win more deals as a team | Avoma Blog. (n.d.). Www.avoma.com. https://www.avoma.com/blog/collaborative-selling

Deal Room: Deal Room Dynamics: Optimizing Virtual Spaces for High Stakes Negotiations. (n.d.). FasterCapital. https://www.fastercapital.com/content/Deal-Room--Deal-Room-Dynamics--Optimizing-Virtual-Spaces-for-High-Stakes-Negotiations.html

Digital 2022 Report Finds Social Media Users Now Equivalent to 58 Percent of the World's Total Population. (2022, January 26). Hootsuite. https://www.hootsuite.com/newsroom/press-releases/digital-2022-report

Effective Sales Prospecting in the Digital Age. (2023, October 16). EMB Global. https://blog.emb.global/effective-sales-prospecting-in-the-digital-age/

Einstein delivers fast service with AI-generated case summaries for bp agents. (n.d.). Salesforce. https://www.salesforce.com/customer-stories/bp/

11 Must-Have Tools For Effective Remote Sales. (2024, March 21). Vainu. https://www.vainu.com/blog/remote-sales-tools/

52 top remote sales tools for your team to absolutely crush it. (n.d.). Close. https://www.close.com/guides-content/remote-sales-tools

Flaherty, M. (2023, May 3). *How Sales Reps Can Adapt to the Hybrid Selling Environment.* RAIN Group Sales Training. https://www.rainsalestraining.com/blog/adapt-to-hybrid-selling

4 Skills You Need to Excel at Virtual Selling (+ Tips). (n.d.). HubSpot Blog. https://blog.hubspot.com/sales/virtual-selling-skills

Hagan-Young, C. (2023, April 6). *CRM vs sales engagement platform: Why you need both.* Sopro. https://sopro.io/resources/blog/crm-vs-sales-engagement-platform-why-you-need-both/

How Heathrow uses data + AI to provide the best airport service in the world. (n.d.). Salesforce. https://www.salesforce.com/resources/customer-stories/heathrow-personalisation-digital-revenue/

One platform, more wishes: Make-A-Wish harnesses data to change lives. (n.d.). Salesforce. https://www.salesforce.com/resources/customer-stories/make-a-wish-data-changes-lives/

Ramakrishna, P. (2021, July 30). *A Guide To Overcoming 21 Most Common Sales Objections.* LeadSquared. https://www.leadsquared.com/learn/sales/handling-overcoming-sales-objections/

Remote Sales Agents Industry Analysis Report: Its Market Size, Share, Trends by Application, Region, Competitive Strategies (2024 - 2031). (n.d.). LinkedIn. https://www.linkedin.com/pulse/remote-sales-agents-industry-analysis-report-its-market-size-3dine/

rockITdata shoots for success with SBA's pandemic programs | U.S. Small Business Administration. (n.d.). SBA. https://www.sba.gov/success-story/rockitdata-shoots-success-sbas-pandemic-programs

Rushe, D. (2021, March 1). *Zoom sees revenues soar 326% year-over-year as office life remains on hold.* The Guardian. https://www.theguardian.com/technology/2021/mar/01/zoom-revenues-results-coronavirus

6 Small Business TikTok Success Stories. (2021, June 17). Wishpond Blog. https://blog.wishpond.com/post/115675438226/small-business-tiktok

Social Selling: What Is Social Selling & Why Is It Important? | LinkedIn Sales Solutions. (2023). Business.linkedin.com. https://business.linkedin.com/sales-solutions/social-selling

Springer, A. (2021, February 3). *20 Virtual Sales Relationship-Building Tips.* RAIN Group Sales Training.

https://www.rainsalestraining.com/blog/20-virtual-sales-relationship-building-tips

10 Must-Have Tools For Effective Remote Sales. (2023). FiveCRM. https://www.fivecrm.com/blog/10-must-have-tools-for-effective-remote-sales/

The Challenger Sale Model: How to Lead the Conversation. (n.d.). Pipedrive. https://www.pipedrive.com/en/blog/challenger-sales-model

The University of Texas Permian Basin. (2020, November 3). *How Much of Communication Is Nonverbal? | UT Permian Basin Online.* Online.utpb.edu. https://online.utpb.edu/about-us/articles/communication/how-much-of-communication-is-nonverbal/

Thomas, G. (2023, September 28). *10 emerging trends shaping the future of SalesOps.* DealHub. https://dealhub.io/blog/sales-operations/10-emerging-trends-shaping-the-future-of-salesops/

2022 State Of Remote Work. (2022). Buffer. https://buffer.com/state-of-remote-work/2022

Waite, H. (2023, October 13). *Virtual Sales Training Programs: 10 Skills Every Seller Needs to Master.* Mindtickle. https://www.mindtickle.com/blog/virtual-sales-training-programs-10-skills-every-seller-needs-to-master/

What are Virtual Sales: Definition, benefits, challenges, and tips. (2022, December 7). Snov.io. https://snov.io/glossary/virtual-sales/

What is a LinkedIn SSI score and how to increase it? (2022, August 11). Sociabble. https://www.sociabble.com/blog/social-selling/linkedin-social-selling-index/

What is BANT? - Breadcrumbs - Revenue Acceleration. (2023, December 1). Breadcrumbs.io. https://breadcrumbs.io/revenuepedia/what-is-bant

www.ingramcontent.com/pod-product-compliance
Lightning Source LLC
Chambersburg PA
CBHW071919210526
45479CB00002B/484